Managing the Crisis in Council Housing

A Report by the Audit Commission

March 1986

LONDON: HER MAJESTY'S STATIONERY OFFICE

ISBN 0 11 701290 4

Table of Contents

Summary

Over the past two years, the Audit Commission has examined the performance of some 400 authorities in England and Wales in managing their stock of 4.8 million dwellings – around one quarter of all households.

This work has revealed a crisis of serious proportions. Some 85% of council-owned dwellings require repairs and improvements – there is a backlog of around £20 billion; and with rents (including Housing Benefit) inadequate generally to keep houses in reasonable condition, the situation is continuing to deteriorate. At the same time, homelessness is increasing. There are a million families on council house waiting lists, and over 175,000 families present themselves as homeless to local authorities every year; yet there are 110,000 empty properties, of which 26,000 have been vacant for more than one year. In addition, the standard of housing management gives cause for concern in a number of authorities where money is being spent on a growing bureaucracy, rather than on better services for tenants.

It is not the purpose of this report to apportion blame for this state of affairs between government, local housing authorities and tenants. All have contributed. Rather, the Commission's concern is to see positive action to correct the situation by all housing authorities and by government as well as by auditors.

Action is being taken at the local level to make better use of the existing stock of council houses. But the overall problem is a much wider one with many facets which cannot sensibly be tackled in isolation. The report therefore covers the range of topics with which housing management needs to be concerned. It looks at the value delivered by over 55,000 people employed in housing management, financial controls, design issues, rent levels, services for the elderly and the homeless, and ways of funding the modernisation of council houses. The report thus provides an overview of the most important steps to be taken to improve housing management; but it does not purport to be exhaustive in every detail and further reports on some topics may be issued later. However, the report does not deal with national housing policy issues which are not a legitimate concern of the Commission, although it covers the effects of these policies.

Action by Housing Authorities

Of course, the position is not the same everywhere. Some authorities have managed the situation better than others; and many of the smaller Shire districts in particular do not suffer so much from the design mistakes and non-traditional building methods promoted by central government in the 1960s. The Commission has concluded that in some 250–300 authorities the problems should be manageable with the resources available locally. In a further 70–80 authorities the situation could be materially improved with better management and using available private sector resources.

However, in approximately 10% of authorities, accounting for some one million dwellings, more public expenditure is likely to be needed either in the form of grants or in the form of tax reliefs and housing benefit. But in these authorities especially, money alone will not be sufficient.

1

If they are not already doing so, all housing authorities should follow the steps set out in this report to:

(i) Improve management of the housing organisation by:
- Making one person, the chief housing officer, accountable for all housing management activities.
- Improving the quality of middle management, by investing in more and better training.
- Decentralising operations to reduce bureaucracy and improve communications with tenants.
- Cutting out unnecessary administration: some 8,000 primarily administrative jobs appear surplus to requirements.
- Endeavouring to get the very best housing managers to work in the most difficult areas. This will require changes to existing terms and conditions of service and new appointment procedures.

(ii) Make better use of the existing stock of council housing, by:
- Up-grading some of the more run-down estates, correcting (or at least not repeating) the design mistakes of the past.
- Minimising the number of empty properties by streamlining letting arrangements – so that the interval between tenancies is no more than three weeks in most cases.
- Providing more hostel accommodation for the homeless and making better use of that which exists, thus reducing very considerably the use of bed and breakfast accommodation for the 75–100,000 households accepted as homeless every year. Apart from other considerations, this is needlessly expensive – as much as £40 a night per family, compared with £12 a night in a reasonable local authority hostel.
- Providing more central alarm services for the increasing number of 'elderly elderly', increasing their sense of security and enabling them to remain in their own homes as long as they are physically able to do so.

(iii) Exercise tighter financial control over housing operations which generate over £3.6 billion in annual rent income and involve expenditure on management, maintenance and finance (debt) charges of over £4 billion a year. This requires:
- Setting rents at appropriate levels. Rents are decided by the local housing authorities; and the Commission's sole concern in this context is to see that local rent policies take account of all the relevant facts and give the appropriate 'signals' to tenants. At present, even though housing benefit is available, rents are generally some £10–15 a week less than would be needed to keep houses in good repair; they rarely reflect the relative attractiveness of properties; and there are unexplained differences between authorities. For instance, rent for a three-bedroom house in Greenwich averaged £15 a week (in April 1985) compared with £28 a week in Wandsworth.
- Taking stronger measures to prevent arrears arising and to collect amounts due. In most authorities, the situation has improved since the Commission published its report on the subject in March 1984. But in some poorly managed authorities, most of them in London, arrears continue to mount. Arrears now total over £250 million; nearly 50 authorities each have arrears over £1 million, just 11 authorities account for £100 million in total.
- Ensuring that the published accounts give an accurate financial picture of local authority housing and that adequate provision is made for maintenance. This will require more widespread

application of the Institute of Housing's recommendations on the use of information technology in housing management, as well as general adoption of the CIPFA guidelines on accounting for central charges, and public reports on the extent of any local maintenance backlog.

(iv) Attract private sector funds to finance needed capital spending. This will mean selling land and property not needed by the authority and reinvesting the proceeds in housing improvements. It should also entail giving local consideration to partnerships with the private sector to attract private funds into public housing, e.g. via building licences, privately funded shared ownership, joint venture developments, mortgages for tenants co-operatives and index-linked mortgages.

Action by Central Government

Central government has a key role to play in making these moves possible. The present combination of controls over individual authorities' capital expenditure on housing, and over design standards for individual projects, represents very detailed involvement in local affairs. For instance, capital allocations are made by Ministers every year to each of 401* housing authorities to the nearest 1/20th of a house. These controls have been an important contributory cause of the present crisis in council housing, as the Commission's report last year, *Capital Expenditure Controls in Local Government in England,* demonstrated.

The Commission considers that rather than seeking detailed central control over the operations of local housing authorities, government should be looking for new ways to attract more private sector finance into public (and particularly council) housing so that consumer preferences can operate. The past practice of giving tenants what they 'ought to want', needs to be replaced by a customer-led approach, providing housing services that people are able (with help as necessary of Housing Benefit) and willing to pay for.

In particular, central controls over local authorities' use of receipts for the sale of capital assets should be relaxed. Borrowing approvals (currently around £1.6 billion per year) and grants for housing purposes should be concentrated on those authorities which cannot be expected to solve the local public housing problems unaided. And the case should be examined for tax reliefs in selected areas of housing stress (e.g. on bond interest, local rates and VAT) as well as that for allowing tenants in high stress areas to apply their *right-to-buy* discounts to any housing purchase. Such measures would help to attract the necessary weight of private funds into the most deprived housing areas.

Finally, a review of the whole area of local authority capital accounting is urgently required, along the lines carried out for the water industry prior to the creation of the water authorities. It makes little sense for government to issue regulations on the form of local authority accounts before the problems associated with creative accounting and provision for the replacement of capital assets have been addressed.

Action by the Commission and its Auditors

The report is based largely on the good practice to be seen now in many authorities. The need is to improve the performance of those authorities who are less proficient in the management of their housing. Auditors have been working with all housing authorities to apply the lessons of this report locally. They will be monitoring progress every six months; and early

---

*Throughout this report the total number of housing authorities is taken to be 401, i.e. excluding the GLC, City of London and the Isles of Scilly.

indications are promising that authorities will take the necessary steps.

The Commission will be publishing a progress report on the situation in inner cities in due course. Later in the year it will be setting out recommendations for improving council housing maintenance – this is a major source of irritation for tenants, and a waste of scarce resources.

* * *

The scale of local housing operations is considerable. The average housing authority manages around 12,000 dwellings with a replacement value of not far short of £250 million. Many are very much bigger than this. The scale of the value improvement potential is correspondingly large. If all authorities successfully apply the recommendations in this report, the benefits will be substantial: perhaps £80–100 million a year could be saved in excessive administration costs; the number of empty council properties could be reduced by 20–25,000; use of bed and breakfast accommodation could be more than 25% lower; rent arrears might be reduced by £100 million, or even more; and given better services, the funds available for maintenance could be increased by as much as £1 billion a year.

Just as important, living conditions for some of the most deprived families could be very substantially improved.

Introduction

1.   'Crisis' is a heavily over-worked word. Yet it is difficult to think of a more appropriate way to describe the state of much of the stock of 4.8 million council-owned dwellings in England and Wales – over a quarter of the nation's dwellings, worth well over £100 billion at replacement cost. A combination of short-sighted national housing policies since the 1960s and shortcomings in local administration has produced a major management challenge in particular in many urban areas:

–   The wrong type of housing. Design faults (e.g. flat roofs, deck access) and problems with new materials and non-traditional construction methods, were not recognised for some time. Partly as a result, many local authorities' estates, accounting for as much as 30% of their total stock in some cases, are now classified as 'difficult to let' even though they are scarcely a decade old.

–   Deteriorating stock. Some 85% of council dwellings in England need repairs and improvements costing almost £5,000 each on average. The backlog of such work on the local authority housing stock has been estimated by the Commission (and by others more recently) at over £20 billion; and it is increasing daily. A recent Department of the Environment (DOE) report suggests that £2 billion is required for essential structural work to load-bearing walls alone. As a result, ghettos for the socially disadvantaged have been created, perpetuating in almost every community the 'them and us' attitudes that constitute such a basic national economic and social handicap.

–   Shortage of housing for rent. If (for example) a newly married couple cannot afford – or do not want – a commercial mortgage they have little alternative to seeking a council house, since the private rented sector has contracted in the last two decades. Since 1960 the number of homes available for rent from private landlords has fallen by some 2.5 million, well in excess of the waiting list for council houses or the current housing shortfall. Partly as a result of the shortage of decent rented accommodation, Britain has a notoriously immobile labour force.

–   Increase in homelessness. The recent *Inquiry into British Housing** cited evidence to show that there is now a deficit of around one million dwellings, after allowance is made for second homes, unfit homes, and those under repair or improvement. There are now over one million people on council house waiting lists; and yet new council building has virtually stopped in many areas. Around 175,000 families present themselves as homeless to local authorities every year. At the same time authorities are demolishing blocks of flats less than 15 years old (with 45 years of debt charges still to run).

---

* Chaired by HRH The Duke of Edinburgh and published by the National Federation of Housing Associations, 1985.

- Unrealistic pricing 'signals'. Despite the shortage of housing for rent, rents are often too low to keep existing dwellings in good repair, still less to finance the necessary expansion. The backlog of maintenance work on council dwellings in England now represents over 5 years rent. Yet, many authorities are still charging rents around half the level necessary to cover the economic cost of the dwelling; and rents rarely reflect the relative 'value' of different dwellings to tenants. As a result tenants are receiving false 'signals' and have unreasonable expectations about the level of service that housing authorities can be expected to afford.

- Weak management control. The number of empty properties can be as high as one in every dozen council dwellings; intervals between lettings of ten weeks are not uncommon; and rent arrears can easily amount to 15–20% of the amount due directly from tenants every year. At the same time, annual administrative costs in some Inner London boroughs now exceed £400 per dwelling. And debt charges are rising.

This is quite a catalogue of 'achievements' for the system to record. It is reflected in unusually high (for local government services) levels of consumer dissatisfaction. A recent MORI poll showed that despite the generally low rents, over 35% of council tenants stated that they were very or fairly dissatisfied with their local housing service, a higher level of dissatisfaction than for any local authority service except road maintenance and street sweeping. And it is reflected in the attitudes to buying: despite discounts of up to 60% on assessed market value less than one-third of tenants not receiving housing benefit have purchased their council house or flat.

2.   These problems have not arisen solely because of local authorities' policies and management. Central government's support for misguided design concepts, grants that encouraged high-rise buildings, administrative problems with housing benefit and rent controls have all contributed to the present problems. More recently, in urban areas especially, declining housing subsidies and rate support grant, tighter restrictions on revenue and capital expenditure, and increasing levels of homelessness have all served to exacerbate a situation which would have been serious enough even in a more favourable era. The trend is likely to continue. Many authorities state that they will have the resources only to provide 'welfare housing', with homeless families taking most, if not all, future relets.

3.   Fortunately, the problems are not universal. Exhibit 1 shows the relative level of housing deprivation in the 401 housing authorities of England and Wales, based on the housing 'Z-scores' calculated by the Department of the Environment. These reflect factors such as the local incidence of over-crowding and lack of basic amenities. The analysis of Z-scores suggests that authorities fall into one of three categories:

(a)   Smaller mainly non-metropolitan (shire) districts where there appear to be few fundamental housing problems and where it is reasonable to expect that the existing resources are adequate to meet local housing needs given sound management.

(b)   Larger authorities, including metropolitan districts and Outer London boroughs, where there are serious but not overwhelming problems, again given sound management.

(c)   Mainly inner-city authorities, many in London, where the social and structural problems with housing are compounded by a local housing shortage and where the management challenge is most acute. As the Exhibit shows, less than 10% of authorities,

Exhibit 1

RELATIVE HOUSING DEPRIVATION
Authorities Housing Z-scores (based on analysis of 1981 census data)

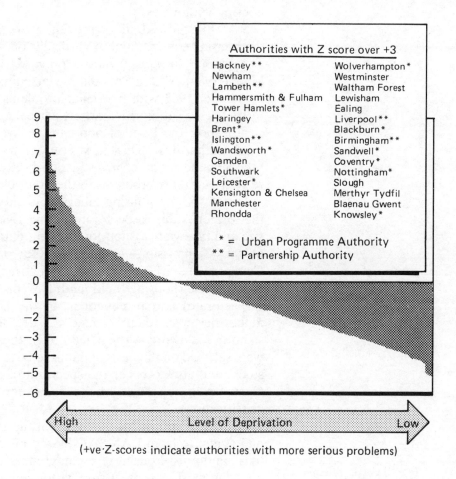

Authorities with Z score over +3	
Hackney**	Wolverhampton*
Newham	Westminster
Lambeth**	Waltham Forest
Hammersmith & Fulham	Lewisham
Tower Hamlets*	Ealing
Haringey	Liverpool**
Brent*	Blackburn*
Islington**	Birmingham**
Wandsworth*	Sandwell*
Camden	Coventry*
Southwark	Nottingham*
Leicester*	Slough
Kensington & Chelsea	Merthyr Tydfil
Manchester	Blaenau Gwent
Rhondda	Knowsley*

* = Urban Programme Authority
** = Partnership Authority

(+ve·Z-scores indicate authorities with more serious problems)

Source: Department of the Environment

accounting for 22% of all council dwellings fall into this category.

The most serious problems described above are thus concentrated in perhaps 30 authorities out of the total*. But every housing authority should be able to benefit from application of the good housing management practice that has been evolved in the more successful authorities (of all types) and is described in the rest of this report.

4. Against this background, the Audit Commission decided that the economy, efficiency and effectiveness of local housing services should be examined. The Commission recognises that there is a close link between the management and maintenance of the housing stock and is therefore engaged in two parallel special studies. This report presents the findings of the work on the supervision and management of the stock. (A complementary report on maintenance will be published towards the end of the year.) At the same time, the Commission is well aware that national and local housing policies exert an important influence on the economy, efficiency and effectiveness of local housing services. However, the Commission has no standing to comment on policy issues. This report is therefore primarily directed to management, and the steps that can usefully

---

* As in subsequent similar exhibits, the situation of each authority is shown separately. Thus, the most deprived authority in housing terms (Hackney) is shown on the left of the chart, with a housing Z-score of +7; and the least deprived (Wokingham) is represented on the extreme right, with a score of −5.

be taken within the existing framework of national and local housing policies. In particular, this report does not consider directly such questions as the amount of public investment in council housing, or tax relief on mortgage interest payments. These questions are for Ministers and Parliament at the national level, and for members of individual local housing authorities.

5.   This study is built on previous work carried out by the Commission in the housing context, and in particular on a study of trends in rent arrears. The report, *Bringing Council Tenants' Arrears Under Control* (HMSO, March 1984), showed overall a worsening trend over the three years to September 1983 with particular problems in some areas. That study was restricted to authorities where arrears were thought to be of most significance: the London boroughs, metropolitan districts, and the larger shire authorities. This new study into supervision and management broadens the scope of investigation both to include all authorities and to relate the arrears problems to the other elements of housing management.

Initial work on housing supervision and management was carried out for the former Audit Inspectorate during 1982. Seven authorities of differing size and type were visited for in-depth data collection. After the formation of the Commission in 1983, a study team was set up consisting of Commission staff, consultants from Ernst & Whinney (who have experience in the housing field and had previously worked for the Audit Inspectorate) and professionals in the housing service. A further eight authorities were then selected for detailed study to widen the original sample. Fieldwork was carried out in the spring of 1984. The authorities were selected on the basis of published data on the range of costs and size of stock, and also to cover the spectrum of authority groupings used by the Commission in much of its value for money work (i.e. the Shaw classification).

Using the knowledge gained from the study work, together with advice and guidance from LAMSAC (based on their experience of research into local authority housing), a comprehensive questionnaire was designed, covering most aspects of supervision and management. This was administered by auditors in nearly all housing authorities in England and Wales as part of the 1984–85 audit round. The response was extremely good – substantially complete questionnaires for 97% of all authorities were returned. Those not responding were either the very small authorities where the opportunities for improvement were judged to be small, or a very few larger authorities which for practical reasons were unable at the time to provide the required information. The Commission was able to call on the resources of its auditors, working to a standard set of terms and definitions. This ensured that the quality and consistency of the data is higher than in any comparable statistics. All the figures shown in this report as originating from the questionnaire survey, including the tables and exhibits, are based on the 97% of responding authorities and are not grossed-up for the non-respondents. This does not introduce any significant bias. The data available represents the most comprehensive picture of local authority housing management yet available, covering the complete range of all types of authority. The content and structure of the questionnaire are described in Appendix A.

6.   This report is therefore based on an analysis of the questionnaire data, supplemented by detailed information collected in visits to the fifteen authorities, and additional examination of particular aspects of interest at other authorities and in the national context. Throughout the study, the appropriate professional and other interested bodies have been consulted including the Local Authority Associations, DOE, the Institute of Housing

(IOH), and trades unions. The study team has also been able to review reports bearing on public housing published recently by the DOE, the *Inquiry into British Housing,* chaired by HRH The Duke of Edinburgh, into the state of the nation's housing stock, as well as the report of the Archbishop of Canterbury's Commission, *Faith in the City*, published in December, 1985.

7. The Audit Commission would like to express particular gratitude to those local authorities which co-operated willingly with the study team during field work for this investigation, as well as to all the 387 authorities which provided information for the completion of the detailed question-naire. Without the time and effort made available to the study team and auditors by members and officers it would not have been possible to carry out this work. When relations between local authorities and central government, and indeed between members and their officers, are often under strain it is particularly gratifying that the Commission has been able to rely on the full co-operation of literally hundreds of authorities of varying size and differing political persuasions. There is a general consensus that things in the housing field cannot go on as they are; and the purpose of this report is to suggest a constructive way forward. As with all the Commission's reports, notwithstanding the many contributions referred to above, responsibility for the conclusions rest with the Commission alone.

8. The Commission has concluded that managing the present crisis in public housing requires four inter-related initiatives particularly in those authorities where housing problems are concentrated.

  (i)   *Management must be improved.* If the council housing function is not properly managed, there can be no realistic prospect for improvement in the situation – however much public money may be made available. More effort needs to be devoted to ensuring that the right managers are in the right place, and that they have appropriate authority to manage. Communications between tenants and councils need to be improved. And available resources need to be concentrated on providing better services, not on financing a burgeoning bureaucracy. Chapter 1 describes the steps that the Commission recommends to achieve these objectives.

  (ii) *More emphasis needs to be placed on providing better services* to tenants. The implied strategy of many authorities appears to be one of charging low rents for minimal service. Many tenants would be prepared to pay more, for better services. Chapter 2 describes some of the ways in which better use can be made of the existing stock of council dwellings.

 (iii) *Financial control should be tightened* over the annual income and expenditure of the order of £4 billion. In the long run, better services must be paid for. Many councils will need to review their rent policies, to ensure that at minimum rents are sufficient to keep the dwellings in good repair. In addition, in many authorities more attention needs to be devoted to collecting rents as well as to management systems. Chapter 3 summarises the action that successful authorities have shown can be taken to strengthen financial control substantially.

 (iv) *New sources of funds to finance improvements in public housing need to be tapped.* The present backlog of repairs and improvements of £20 billion cannot be financed by the public sector alone – even if government is willing to see a marked increase in central and local government borrowing. Apart from any macro-economic considerations, the eventual annual interest costs – of perhaps as much as £2 billion a year – would be insupportable: the total cost of primary teachers' salaries is not much more than £2 billion a year. New approaches must be found to attract private finance into public housing. But these approaches will not be sufficient to meet the needs of inner cities without some publicly financed pump-priming, and re-direction of existing grants and borrowing approvals. Chapter 4 discusses some of the recent initiatives in this area that have been tried and which are worth further consideration.

9.   Collectively, these steps cover all the main initiatives needed to improve housing management. Obviously, the report cannot be exhaustive: each step could well be the subject of a separate Commission report in due course. Equally obviously, it will be apparent that the initiatives described above cannot sensibly be considered in isolation. Better management is a precondition for improving services; in turn, services can only be improved significantly if there are the resources to pay for them – which implies adequate financial control. The Commission therefore regards the initiatives proposed in this report as an integrated package. It is not offering an *a la carte* menu, from which recommendations can sensibly be selected according to the reader's ideological taste.

1. Improving housing management

10. Managing the national stock of council-owned dwellings is a demanding management task, at the heart of efforts to deal with the problems of urban deprivation. At many local authorities in England and Wales housing represents the largest asset and is also the largest service provided both in terms of expenditure and staffing. This is true of most of the Shire district councils and Inner London boroughs where housing can account for 40–45% of gross annual expenditure – and around £40 million in annual income. Even in the metropolitan districts and the Outer London boroughs, housing can account for 20–25% of expenditure, particularly where there are large concentrations of high density estates.

11. Although the number of local authority dwellings has fallen to below 5 million recently (mainly as a result of sales to sitting tenants), and there are now fewer than 23,000 new council houses being started each year in England and Wales, local authority housing still accounts for over one-quarter of the total housing stock. Even excluding land values, and taking a conservative estimate of market value of £20,000 per dwelling, the asset value of the nation's council house stock approaches £100 billion. In replacement cost terms, the value would be substantially more than this.

Exhibit 2

TOTAL SUPERVISION AND MANAGEMENT EXPENDITURE, FY 1984

£ per dwelling

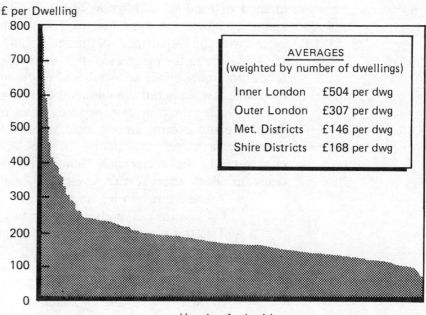

Source: Audit Commission Survey, 1985

12.   The management of this asset is clearly of major importance in economic as well as social terms. Excluding maintenance and loan charges, towards £1 billion per year is spent on the day-to-day processes of providing a housing management service to the authorities' tenants. In crude terms this represents almost £200 per dwelling per year; but the figures from authority to authority range from £70 to £770 a year per dwelling, as Exhibit 2 shows. Table 1 shows the average costs by class of authority. It is divided into two main categories, using the normal CIPFA definitions: general supervision and management costs for services to all tenants (such as rent collection and accounting), and special costs relating to services which are for some, rather than all, tenants (such as caretaking and cleaning).

Table 1: SUPERVISION AND MANAGEMENT COSTS PER DWELLING, 1983–4
Weighted average by class of authority

	Shire Districts	Met Districts	Outer London Boroughs	Inner London Boroughs
	£	£	£	£
General expenditure	£102/dwelling	84	166	236
Special expenditure	66	62	141	268
Total	168	146	307	504
Elements of the total expenditure (%):-				
Central Establishment charges	29	19	19	13
Insurance	2	2	2	1
Sales Administration	6	3	4	1
Central Heating	8	8	15	17
Caretaking/Cleaning	1	6	14	16
Services for the Elderly	17	12	7	3
Maintenance of Open Spaces	7	8	5	4
Provision for the Homeless	3	1	8	9
Other general expenditure	23	34	20	28
Other special expenditure	4	7	6	8
[No. of authorities included	321	36	19	11
% of all authorities	96	100	95	92]

These figures can be contrasted with the management costs of housing associations, although the figures are not strictly comparable because the method of funding is different and many housing associations draw on voluntary labour, to some extent. The standard management allowances agreed with the Department of the Environment for housing associations in 1984–85 were in the range £155–195 per dwelling. The bottom of the range relates to a new build, non-sheltered dwelling outside London; the top of the range is a sheltered rehabilitated dwelling in London.

13.   During the course of the study, the Commission has recognised the great diversity existing among local authorities in terms of the number of dwellings managed, the nature of the stock, the types of problems encountered, the social and demographic conditions and the policy decisions which affect service levels. For example:

- Around one housing authority in five has under 5,000 dwellings; but less than 20 housing authorities manage over 40,000.
- Two-thirds of housing authorities have no tower blocks at all; but 25 have more than 50.
- 155 authorities in the Commission's survey have fewer than 500 dwellings for old people; but 25 have over 2,500.
- In nearly half the 387 authorities surveyed, council owned dwellings account for less than 25% of the total; but in 25 authorities, council owned dwellings account for over half the local dwellings.

14. Expenditure on housing management is increasing at a faster rate than general inflation, as measured by the retail prices index. Exhibit 3 shows that in real terms the cost of managing council housing has risen by 30–40% over the six years to 1983–84. At the same time the number of dwellings is now 4% lower than six years ago, having reached a peak in the early 1980s. The Exhibit shows the overall figures for all authorities in England and Wales but the trends are only marginally different by class of authority. Since 1977–78 general expenditure has increased in real terms by 44% in London and 28% in the shire districts for example. As a result, in many authorities expenditure on supervision and management of the housing stock now exceeds that on annual maintenance. Few authorities spend more than £250 per dwelling every year on response maintenance; but Table 2 below shows that a number of authorities spend more than this on the supervision and management of their housing stock.

Exhibit 3

TRENDS IN HOUSING SUPERVISION AND MANAGEMENT EXPENDITURE, FY 1978-84
Adjusted for inflation (FY 1978 = 100)

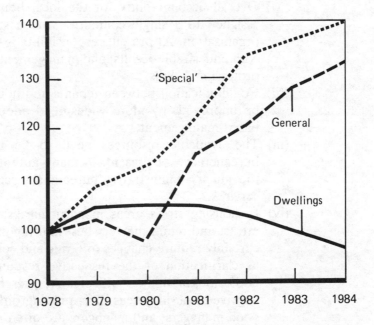

Source: CIPFA Housing Revenue Account Statistics

Table 2: HOUSING AUTHORITY SUPERVISION AND MANAGEMENT COSTS, 1983–4
Number of Authorities

	London Boroughs	Shire Districts
£250–350/dwelling	7	12
£351–450	9	3
£451–550	1	1
Over £550	5	—
	22	16

The 38 authorities in question (less than 10% of the total) account for some 13% of all council housing. There is no metropolitan district with expenditure greater than £250 per dwelling.

15.   It is symptomatic of the lack of information about council housing that it is not possible to provide an analysis of the causes of the increases shown in the Exhibit. Professionals in the housing field cite a number of possible reasons for expenditure to have risen on this scale including an expansion in the provision of services for the elderly, the introduction of the Housing Benefit scheme (with perhaps under-recovery of staffing and administration costs); an increase in central establishment charges; deteriorating stock requiring greater expenditure on maintenance and improvement, with the associated additional administration costs and staffing; fuel price increases above the rate of general inflation (and perhaps also resulting in greater deficits on heating charges); increasing homelessness and a greater need for housing advice and welfare; and the effect of the introduction of *right-to-buy* legislation under the 1980 *Housing Act*.

16.   Whatever the reasons for the increase, it is clear that investing large amounts of additional money in housing management – expenditure in the year to end March 1984 was £250 million in real terms higher than six years earlier (at 1984 wage and salary levels) – has not produced a satisfactory situation either for tenants or ratepayers in many authorities, who have seen the value of their assets decline even as the cost of housing management has increased. The Commission has concluded that four steps are needed to strengthen council house management:

(i) Overall accountability for the local housing service needs to be assigned to a single committee and a strengthened management organisation. At present responsibility is often unduly fragmented, with undesirable results; and management often lacks the necessary professional skills.

(ii) Communication between tenants and housing authorities needs to be improved, by more widespread adoption of area and estate-based management.

(iii) The available resources need to be invested in services not bureaucracy. At present, in many authorities there appears to be too much administrative bureaucracy, combined with inadequate services.

(iv) In housing stress areas in particular, steps need to be taken to attract and retain the very best housing managers. This will almost certainly require changes to terms and conditions of service as well as clarification of the respective responsibilities of members of authorities and their officers. At present, in many of the most deprived housing areas, it is proving difficult to recruit and keep good managers; and managers are often not free to manage.

The rest of this chapter discusses each of these steps in turn.

APPROPRIATE ORGANISATION, STRUCTURE AND RESPONSIBILITIES

17.   Very few authorities operate in exactly the same way. Some have a highly centralised housing department; others are almost entirely decentralised. Some have all the housing functions under the direct control of a chief housing officer; others operate with the financial aspects outside the housing department, under the treasurer; yet others have no separate housing organisation at all, typically with the treasurer in control of the management of all council housing. The use of computers also varies widely. Even the range and type of housing services offered show great differences. There are three main issues to be resolved in respect of the local organisation structure for housing:

(i) In respect of smaller authorities, the minimum size for a separate housing department and the extent to which financial matters (rent collection and accounting, Housing Benefit administration, arrears control) rest with the finance department.

(ii) In respect of larger authorities, the degree of decentralisation both in terms of the size of the area management unit and scope of its powers.

(iii) The extent to which housing management exercises control over central establishment and other charges.

Each of these is discussed briefly below.

Consolidated management responsibility

18. A unified housing function is much to be preferred. It is less confusing for tenants to have a single point of contact with the authority. And, perhaps more important in this context, there is clear managerial responsibility and accountability. Yet 12 small housing authorities have no separate housing department (their average stock size is less than 4,000). In 108 authorities the treasurer is responsible at least for rent collection, rent accounting, arrears recovery and housing benefit; and in these cases the average stock size is below 8,000. Where financial management is assigned separately, authorities ought to ensure that there are worthwhile economies to balance the obvious disadvantages in terms of fragmented responsibility.

19. However, consolidated local management responsibility will only make sense if sufficient people of the required calibre and commitment are available to staff the organisation. More effort needs to be devoted generally to upgrading the quality of housing management. Simply appointing the right person and giving him (or her) the necessary freedom to manage will not suffice of itself to improve local housing management. These are necessary, but not sufficient steps. The professionalism of housing management needs to be enhanced generally; and the Commission welcomes the initiatives in this area that have been launched by the Institute of Housing. However, it would be idle to pretend that housing managers at all levels have the appropriate professional knowledge and management skills.

- Fewer than 2,500 staff within local government housing organisations have the recognised professional qualification in this field, from the Institute of Housing; this represents less than one qualified housing officer for every 2,000 dwellings (worth some £50 million in replacement costs) in the local authority housing stock in England and Wales. Although some staff in addition hold other relevant technical qualifications (e.g. in building and surveying), the overall picture is still less than satisfactory.

- In-service training is limited. Even in one of the better managed housing organisations within local government, average training time for third tier managers amounts to less than two days a year per person.

- Typically, estate management is the responsibility of relatively young and inexperienced people who are newcomers to the estate for which they are responsible. Only a very small fraction of estate management staff have a relevant housing qualification.

20. In staffing terms, authorities should focus on quality, not quantity; and this attitude needs to be reflected in the terms and conditions of service. And, generally, there needs to be more investment in in-service training. A target of 10 days a year per person for the top four tiers of housing management is not unreasonable: this is the amount of off-station training every year for every fireman in a typical brigade, and would be regarded as reasonable in well-managed private sector organisations. Of course, this will cost money. But the sums involved will be trivial in relation both to the scale of the problem facing council housing and to the replacement cost of the assets – a large housing authority could well have housing stock worth in excess of £750 million at replacement cost.

21. Indeed, there is a case for setting up a housing staff college to provide a focal point for management training and development and for research into management issues within the public housing field. At present there are such colleges for the Police (Bramshill) and the Fire Service (Moreton-in-Marsh). The annual cost of operating the latter is under £7 million a year; yet annual expenditure on fire services amounts to less than 10% of gross expenditure on council housing in England and Wales.

Area management

22. In larger authorities, an area-based housing organisation structure is generally appropriate. For the 129 authorities with more than 10,000 dwellings, 65% have some form of area-based management and where this is found it covers on average 7,200 dwellings per area (about 50% of such areas are within the range of 4,300 and 8,500). The larger centralised housing authorities should consider introducing greater delegation to the area level. The following functions can be devolved to managers with areas of 4–5,000 dwellings:

- Cash office and the organisation of any door-to-door rent collection service;
- Arrears control either by generic estate management staff or by specialists;
- Void inspections;
- (Pre) viewing and letting of property;
- Tenant liaison;
- Receipt of repairs requests (although 85% of such requests are by telephone or post).

The definition of suitable areas in particular authorities will be influenced by the spread of the authority and established communities within it. The study found no evidence to show that area management requires more staff than in a centralised authority of similar size.

23. A number of urban and inner-city authorities are attempting a much greater degree of decentralisation, often associated with the devolvement of other functions such as social services and planning. In principle, the Commission favours maximum delegation of authority and responsibility as far down the line as possible. Delegation to the estate level can involve an increase in staff numbers, as some scale advantages are foregone. But it could also lead to a higher level of service and greater tenant involvement and satisfaction; and, in many cases, the authorities which most need estate-level management are already over-staffed at the centre and could therefore afford to re-deploy some of their existing staff resources.

24. Whatever the degree of any decentralisation, a clear definition is required of the powers of area management and any associated housing committee. These can range from a mere geographical split of staff to devolved area budgets with local power of virement. Exhibit 4 describes the stages of decentralisation and the resultant responsibilities of the local manager. It is based on a classification scheme developed as part of a study being carried out by Building Use Studies Ltd commissioned by the Royal Institute of Public Administration.

Control over central charges

25. Charges to the housing accounts for central services (such as personnel, legal, computer, payroll etc.) can be substantial. Typically between 15% and 20% of a housing department's annual expenditure on supervision and management can be accounted for by such charges. In some authorities the figure is very much more than this, as Exhibit 5 demonstrates. Viewed in terms of an average cost of central establishment charges (CEC) per dwelling, there are equally large variations from

Exhibit 4

STAGES OF HOUSING MANAGEMENT DECENTRALISATION IN LOCAL AUTHORITIES

STAGE OF DECENTRALISATION	DRIVING FORCE	RESPONSIBILITIES OF LOCAL MANAGER	IMPLICATIONS
Locally dispersed offices or personnel	Political, to improve services to (frustrated) tenants	Little or no devolution of management responsibility at the local level	Ineffective unless quickly followed by change in information systems and work organisation. Disillusionment at lack of service improvement
Provision of local access to centrally-based information system	Information Technology, to improve existing centralised services	Re-active role; improved management	May lead gradually to more use of management information
Delegation to local (area/estate) level. Development of limited budgetary responsibility. Some local organisation eg. Estate-based repair teams	Managerial, to mitigate the disbenefits of scale in housing organisations. Many authorities are approaching this stage, through pilot schemes eg. Priority Estates Projects:	More local responsibility and accountability. Creates demand for better local access to available management information	Encourages local managers to manage and to demand more responsibility. Requires computer-based systems
Full decentralisation: local offices as autonomous cost centres, housing, social services, remedial education and health professionals	But, no local authority has yet decentralised completely	Local manager is responsible for expenditure on staff resources and overheads, and has budgetary control. Rent income and repairs expenditure under local manager's control	Depends on central support services to local managers (especially information) and requires changes in committee structure and responsibilities

Exhibit 5

CENTRAL ESTABLISHMENT CHARGES TO HOUSING, FY 1984

CEC as % General and Special Housing Management expenditure

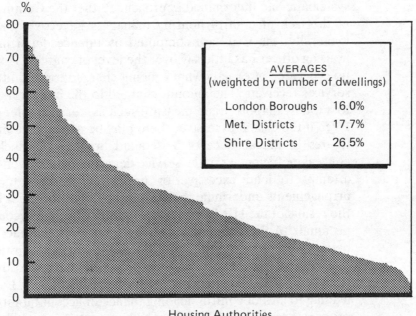

AVERAGES
(weighted by number of dwellings)

London Boroughs   16.0%
Met. Districts   17.7%
Shire Districts   26.5%

Housing Authorities

Source: Audit Commission Survey, 1985

authority to authority. Interpretation of the figures requires care, particularly as a result of the many different organisational structures employed by authorities; but these factors do not by any means explain all of the observed variations in central costs.

26.   CEC include the cost of central functions such as personnel, salaries and wages, and usually office overheads (including debt charges, heating, lighting, telephones, etc). Similarly, nearly all authorities will have legal specialists outside the housing department, and paid for by the CEC in respect of time spent on housing-related matters. The allocation of many other functions is less uniform; but the following list shows those 'housing' functions which are carried out outside the housing department in many authorities and hence may also be the subject of CEC:

- Financial matters (e.g. rent collection and accounting, arrears recovery, Housing Benefit administration).
- Council house sales administration including mortgage applications, surveyors' and legal costs.
- Capital project management.
- Housing research and preparation of DOE Housing Investment Programme (HIP) and other returns.
- Computing, particularly where the council operates a central mainframe computer.

Even after making adjustments to the figure for CEC shown in the accounts to take account of the organisational differences, there still remain wide variations in the CEC per dwelling. Two small authorities studied, of very similar size (5,500 dwellings approximately) had CEC of £13 and £32 per dwelling respectively, even after all reasonable adjustments. One much larger authority showed an average cost of £75 per dwelling charged to the Housing Revenue Account (HRA). Even allowing for the necessarily approximate nature of the adjustments, and for the possibly inaccurate or incomplete reporting of the original figures in the accounts, such differences raise important questions. After all, the difference could easily amount to £1 million a year or more in a large housing authority.

27.   The key issue however is not the actual figures themselves, which may or may not be an over-statement of the true cost of the services to the housing department – although experience in the private sector suggest that most overhead costs can be reduced by 15–20%, given a sufficiently systematic and determined approach. Rather the Commission is concerned at the lack of control housing managers have over the housing budget. Generally, the CEC are computed by finance department staff. A chief housing officer has little say over the level of charges. He (or she) may have no clear idea of exactly what is being charged for and little choice over the services received. The amount charged to the budget may well be *pro rata* to a totally inappropriate measure such as, for example, gross expenditure. Even if the cost is excessive, there may be no opportunity to challenge the figures in the absence of a detailed breakdown. Such a situation may conceal inefficiencies in the service departments, or even worse a deliberate attempt to load excessive or unjustified charges to the HRA. Such arrangements undermine the accountability of the chief housing officer for the results of the HRA, which is a statutory trading account. They may also be unfair to the tenants in denying them the assurance that their rent is being spent properly on the purposes for which it is intended.

28.   The Commission considers that all charges to the HRA should at least be open to challenge by the chief housing officer. Lack of information, leading to lack of control, leading to lack of accountability is contrary to the principles of sound organisation and is inconsistent with the achievement of value-for-money. The solution is for chief housing officers to be provided

with an itemised account of the charges arising from each central department. This should include details of staff numbers, man-days allocated, and other costs directly incurred. Even if these are only estimates they would be better than no information at all. It would then be possible to challenge the appropriateness of charges and for direct comparisons to be made with outside suppliers, e.g. for legal, architects' or computer services.

29.   A particular problem often arises over costs of maintenance of open spaces, and charged to the HRA. Although generally thought not to be of major significance, in fact large sums are involved: total expenditure approached £60 million in 1983–84, almost as much as on caretaking and cleaning. In many authorities more is spent on HRA open space maintenance than on services for the elderly. Two problems are apparent. First, as with CEC, a chief housing officer often has little opportunity to challenge the amount set against the housing budget, because the management information is inadequate. Secondly, tenants may be paying for services which should be the responsibility of other departments, such as leisure and amenities (e.g. public open space) and highways (e.g. roadside verges).

30.   Comparison of unit costs for maintenance of open spaces is difficult, partly because many authorities have no accurate information on the area maintained, and partly because the cost of maintenance depends on the nature of the open space – mowing of areas of grass can be expected to be cheaper than maintaining flower beds, for example. Similarly, one large area should be less costly to maintain than the same area in smaller plots. As a result, less than half of the authorities were able to supply information on the area maintained on behalf of the housing committee. This in itself highlights the difficulty a chief housing officer has in controlling expenditure. Nonetheless, it has been possible to make some comparisons which at least put the potential savings into context. For those authorities where the information was available:

- Annual maintenance costs varied between £1,200 and £4,000 per hectare for the middle 50% of authorities;
- A typical authority has 170 hectares; so in an authority with costs per hectare at the top of the range, spending would approach £500,000 a year more than an authority with costs at the bottom of this range;
- The cost variation among authorities reflects service levels (e.g. how often grass is cut, etc.) the nature of the landscaping, the size of the plots, and other design and access considerations. In many cases some of these factors are, at least in the short term, outside the control of the local chief housing officer. However, there are factors which can be controlled and savings to be achieved e.g. by method changes, improved labour productivity and less labour-intensive grounds layouts.

* * *

At the very least, the detailed cost information on what the housing department is obtaining for its money in the various central charges should be available to the chief housing officer and the local Housing Committee when budgets are being prepared. At present, this appears to be the exception, not the rule.

IMPROVING COMMUNICATIONS BETWEEN TENANTS AND AUTHORITIES

31.   Particularly in large housing authorities, the council can seem remote and impersonal to tenants. Even area managers with responsibility for perhaps 5,000 dwellings will often appear to have no time for the concerns of individual tenants. In such circumstances, it is easy to see how a

vicious circle could be established:

- Tenants do not know who to contact directly, so they resort to putting complaints in writing and telephoning 'the office';
- Messages are lost and a correspondence backlog builds up;
- Preoccupied with a paper backlog, staff are less responsive to immediate problems; and (naturally) tend to respond to pressure from the more assertive tenants and members of the authority, on the 'oil the squeaky wheel' principle.
- This simply leads to a worsening of the situation, distortion of priorities and extra costs, as voids and the resulting vandalism increase.

32. Private developers have long recognised the need to have a local office on site. An estate manager should be the first point of contact between the tenant and the authority. The manager should be responsible for: inspections of estates and property, dealing with tenants' disputes, tenant consultation, liaison with tenants' associations, general housing advice, assistance with mutual exchanges and assistance during modernisation programmes. It is often sensible to combine these tasks with arrears prevention, void control and in some cases, rent collection. But, when a local estate-based housing management service is provided, it is important that the purely estate management activities are not neglected in favour of apparently more urgent day to day matters.

33. Despite the obvious importance of the estate management role, it receives apparently relatively little attention. While it is difficult to estimate exactly, the total annual expenditure on estate management itself, as defined above, is probably not more than £25 million i.e. less than £5 a year per dwelling. It has contracted in recent years because of: the reduction in door-to-door rent collection, the increasing specialisation of many housing departments, emphasis on other activities (e.g. the growing numbers of arrears cases), and the pressure to contain staff and cost levels. Almost a quarter of the authorities covered in the Commission's survey devoted negligible effort to estate management.

34. This contraction continues despite the growing problems on certain estates and of local authority housing generally, as described earlier. The Commission asked authorities to identify all staff currently working on purely estate management activities, isolating the time spent on these activities from rent collection, arrears control etc. (Appendix A defines precisely the categorisation of staff used by the questionnaire). Total estate management staff amount to the full-time equivalent (f.t.e.) of only 2,700, not much more than one for every 2,000 dwellings overall. In many individual authorities, there are more staff engaged in waiting list administration and lettings than in the arguably far more important tasks of estate management. Although many authorities put greater emphasis on estate management than the above averages imply (both in terms of cost and staffing), the effort in many others is inadequate to reflect the need to encourage closer authority/tenant relationships and to halt further deterioration in, for example, arrears and the condition of the stock generally. At minimum, housing authorities should consider the local case for delegating more responsibility to existing housing areas.

35. Estates can also be improved by effective tenant consultative procedures, which many (but by no means all) authorities operate in accordance with the requirements of the 1980 *Housing Act*. Although it may not always be easy to engender the necessary enthusiasm, the experience of authorities such as Doncaster shows that tenants' committees can:

- Ensure that communal facilities are maintained.

- Identify low cost improvements, e.g. entry phones, car parking, anti-vandal measures.
- Welcome new tenants and provide them with information on the location of services and any communal facilities.
- Most importantly, encourage the necessary sense of joint ownership.

36.   Indeed, it is the view of many authorities and the Commission that a high level of tenant involvement is essential if local housing services are to deliver the type and quality of housing which tenants really want. To this end, Rochdale proposes to establish a network of 15 local housing management committees (one for every 1,500 council owned dwellings) comprising: the councillors for the wards in question, the Chairman of the Borough's Housing Services Committee (or his nominee) and six tenants in good standing nominated by the recognised tenants' associations. The local Member(s) of Parliament would be a visiting member. The committees would have the following main duties:

- To consider the needs of their estates and of the people who live on them.
- To prepare and propose to the Housing Services Committee each year estate management expenditure budgets, under 15 different headings, covering: staffing, different categories of maintenance, void repairs and losses, grass cutting and environmental maintenance.
- To monitor and control the approved budgets for their estates. The Committee has powers to shift funds between different budget headings, provided that the overall estate budgets are not exceeded.
- To promote positive dialogue and co-operation between the residents of the estates, the staff responsible for local estate management and the elected representatives concerned.

37.   The approach adopted by some authorities to rehabilitate run down estates is to create estate-based management teams. Some authorities have done this with DOE support through the Priority Estates Project (PEP). The work so far carried out on localised housing management suggests that there are benefits in bringing a level of management much closer to individual estates or to smaller districts. Significant improvements have been seen in void levels and other indicators. Although a full assessment of costs and benefits has not yet been completed, some work has been carried out to monitor progress. (See for example: *Local Housing Management – A Priority Estates Project Survey:* DOE, 1984). Some of the benefits of more localised management may be achieved by greater delegation of powers to existing area offices.

INVESTMENT IN SERVICES, NOT BUREAUCRACY

38.   A total of over 55,000 people is employed within housing management in local authorities in England and Wales, at an annual cost well in excess of £600 million. About 20,000 provide special services e.g. wardens, caretakers and cleaners; but the balance is occupied in administrative duties. Obviously, it is important that these staff resources are devoted to improving services, and not simply to shuffling paper. Some Inner London authorities employ approaching 1,000 people in general supervision and management – excluding those engaged in maintenance. The Commission has therefore analysed the information from different housing authorities to identify:

(a)   Those factors outside an authority's control that appear to influence staffing levels.

(b) 'Good practice' levels of staffing for particular housing management services, taking into account relevant local conditions and the requirements of efficiency and effectiveness.

Table 3 below summarises the breakdown of housing management staff by function and class of authority; and Exhibit 6 shows the wide range of staffing in relation to the size of the local housing stock. Staff performing housing functions in other departments are included, while staff in housing departments but not involved in housing management tasks are excluded (e.g. post-inspection maintenance staff).

Table 3: ANALYSIS OF HOUSING SUPERVISION AND MANAGEMENT STAFF, 1983–4

	Shire Districts %	Met. Districts %	Outer London Boroughs %	Inner London Boroughs %	Memo: TOTAL STAFF
Rents (collection, accounting, etc.)	20	21	17	10	11,200
Waiting lists and lettings	6	7	6	7	3,100
Services for the elderly	29	19	13	4	12,300
Caretaking and cleaning	5	16	20	35	7,500
Estate management	4	4	7	10	2,700
Housing advice and homelessness	3	4	6	4	2,500
Repairs administration	11	10	11	7	5,700
Other (inc. administration)	22	19	20	23	12,000
TOTAL	100	100	100	100	
Memo: TOTAL STAFF	29,100	15,000	5,800	7,100	57,000
Per 1000 dwellings	11	12	16	22	
[Lowest 25%	9	9	13	16]	

Exhibit 6

GENERAL SUPERVISION AND MANAGEMENT STAFF
Staff per 1000 dwellings

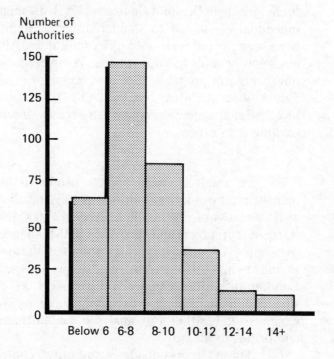

Number of Authorities

Source: Audit Commission Survey, 1985

22

Certain staff, notably wardens, hostel staff, and caretakers and cleaners do not service all dwellings and therefore distort the broad averages shown above. Nonetheless, the table also shows the particular problems in Inner London: total supervision and management staffing per dwelling is very nearly double the level in metropolitan districts – and represent an additional 1,750 full-time administrative posts.

39.   Variations in staffing levels within housing departments can be due to such factors as different methods of service delivery, e.g. the level of door-to-door rent collection and the extent of computerisation; the nature of the stock and the socio-demographic characteristics of the tenants and those seeking council housing; local authorities' choice of different levels of service; and relative economy and efficiency and/or effectiveness. The analysis has sought to identify the relative importance of these factors in explaining the variation. The characteristics of tenants and potential tenants and, in the short term at least, the nature of the stock are substantially outside the immediate control of the councils concerned. The emphasis of the analysis has therefore been to attempt to allow for such factors so that the remaining variation may be ascribed to local choice about the level of service and relative economy, efficiency and effectiveness.

40.   Rather than attempt to analyse the total housing staff the Commission has examined in turn the major elements of staffing concerned with housing supervision and management. The statistical analysis method used is explained in Appendix B. In general the analysis has been able to explain a considerable part of the variation identified. Nonetheless there is a substantial residue which appears to be due to the different levels of service that are to be found and to variations in economy and efficiency. In many instances the latter factor was most important, suggesting many local opportunities to improve value for money. In total, the analysis suggests that staffing levels could be reduced perhaps by as much as 8,000 if all authorities were able to operate as economically and efficiently as the best quarter in each category of authorities. The staffing levels suggested are compatible with recommended good practice set out later. The rest of this chapter therefore deals in turn with the appropriate local staffing levels for letting and void control, rent collection and accounting, caretaking and cleaning, services for the elderly and the homeless. All authorities with staffing above the levels suggested should launch local enquiries to determine why they are not able to match the performance of the good practice authorities and/or whether additional staffing is reflected in above-average levels of service.

Letting property

41.   Administration in the three related areas of the management of the waiting and transfer lists, the letting of properties, and void control has been examined in order to identify the potential that may exist for more economic staffing levels without prejudice to standards of service. An apparently considerable variation in productivity has been identified. Exhibit 7 shows the variation in the numbers of staff devoted to the administration of the waiting and transfer lists. There are considerable variations by class of authority. The average staff per 1,000 applicants varies from 1.7 in the metropolitan districts to over twice this in Inner London, with an overall average of 2.5. There are similarly wide variations within each authority class.

42.   Analysis shows that waiting list staffing levels are not affected by the total list size but rather by the number of new applicants to the list, the total number of visits made and socio-demographic factors. Even taking account of these explanatory factors, there is still a considerable inter-authority variation in staffing. Many large authorities manage waiting lists

Exhibit 7

ADMINISTRATION OF WAITING AND TRANSFER LISTS, FY 1984

(Applications/staff member/week)

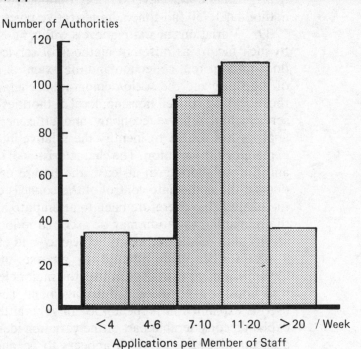

Source: Audit Commission Survey, 1985

with fewer than 1.4 full-time equivalent staff per thousand new applicants. Yet over 150 authorities have staffing 50% or more above this level. If every authority operated the staffing levels that have already been achieved by a quarter of authorities, total staff resources devoted to letting property could be reduced by nearly 1,000, without any necessary reduction in standards of service. There is also a considerable variation in the numbers of void control staff. There were on average 1.4 staff for every hundred voids (excluding those awaiting sale or demolition) – i.e. over three staff days per void. But this figure varied from 0.4 to 1.6 for the middle 50% of authorities even after allowing for external factors. No additional reasons were found to explain this variation.

With the assistance of auditors, authorities are now reviewing local staffing levels for these functions to determine the reasons why staffing should be above good practice levels.

Rent collection and accounting

43. Staff concerned with the rent income include those responsible for rent collection, cash offices, rent accounting, housing benefit administration and control over tenants' arrears. Table 4 below shows the average performance in different classes of authority:

Table 4: RENT COLLECTION AND ACCOUNTING STAFFING, 1983–4
Full-time equivalents

	Shire Districts	Met. Districts	Outer London Boroughs	Inner London Boroughs
Rent collection/1,000 payments:				
– Door-to-door	3.1	3.0	4.9	—
– Cash office	1.7	2.4	2.9	2.6
Rent accounting/1,000 new lets	4.1	5.2	7.3	7.1
Housing Benefit admin/1,000 recipients	1.2	1.0	1.8	2.1
Arrears/1,000 cases	1.3	1.7	1.7	1.1

44. There are very wide differences in staffing levels in the same class of authority to carry out apparently similar functions: differences of two to one between the low-staff quarter of authorities in a particular class and the high-staff quarter are routine. In each case, multiple regression analyses were carried out as described in Appendix B to see whether external conditions explain a significant amount of the variation shown in the table. These analyses showed for example that:

(a) Neither the density of dwellings whose rent is collected door-to-door nor socio-demographic factors (such as the level of overcrowding, the numbers sharing basic amenities and the number of ethnic households) were found to affect the speed of door-to-door collection.

(b) The number of cash offices was not found to be significant in determining staffing per 1,000 payments.

(c) The number of new accounts opened was found to give a better explanation of staffing variations in rent accounting than the total number of transactions (presumably because the volume of transactions generally more affects the computer rather than the staff workload).

(d) The number of arrears control staff in post depends both on the number of arrears cases and the size of the debt.

45. Many authorities have been able to achieve staffing levels of 1.8 rent collection staff per 1,000 door-to-door payments, 1.0 per 1,000 cash office payments and 2.8 rent accounting staff per 1,000 new lets, while achieving respectable standards of service. Many of these good practice authorities have relatively high housing Z-scores and thus have some difficult local housing problems to cope with. If all authorities were able to achieve these levels, then staffing for rent accounting and collection would fall by some 2,200 from the current level of 11,200.

Of course there may be reasons which cannot be revealed even by the Commission's very detailed survey, why a particular local authority cannot achieve these levels. For example door-to-door rent collection is a more onerous task if only a small proportion of tenants pay by this method and they are spread evenly, and thinly, across the authority. The Commission's auditors are working with local authority staff in order to identify such local circumstances. Local managers, both members and officers, in authorities with higher staffing levels than those referred to above should investigate to see whether there are either unusual local circumstances or better services to justify the additional public investment involved.

Caretaking and cleaning

46. These services relate only to a part of the total housing stock: caretaking, primarily to tower blocks and cleaning to the communal areas of estates. Many of the smaller authorities do not have any such dwellings and hence do not employ caretakers or cleaners. Comparisons of staffing levels (and cost) must therefore be related to the number of dwellings receiving the services, not to the total stock. There are wide variations in both the unit cost per dwelling serviced and in the number of caretakers/cleaners per 1,000 dwellings, as illustrated below in Table 5.

Much of this variation may reflect the different levels of service provided. Some caretakers, for example, also have responsibility for collecting rents, and play an active part in estate management. Similarly the design of estates and the size of blocks also influences the cost and staffing. Nevertheless out of total national expenditure on caretaking and cleaning of over £70 million a year there are opportunities for substantial savings without compromising service standards. Authorities should review regularly the level of service required in relation to the workload of individual

Table 5: CARETAKING AND CLEANING STAFFING, 1983–4
F.t.e. per 1,000 dwellings serviced

	Shire Districts	Met. Districts	Outer London Boroughs	Inner London Boroughs	All Authorities
average	6.3	8.4	5.7	7.6	6.4
lowest 25%*	5.6	6.7	5.1	7.3	6.0
highest 25%	13.9	12.7	9.2	10.1	12.7

* Throughout this report, reference is made to the 'lowest' and 'highest' 25% of authorities. These are the quartile authorities, *not* the average of the lowest and highest 25% of authorities. Thus, the reduction in staffing levels referred to above could be achieved if all authorities match the current performance of 25% of authorities in the same class, after appropriate adjustments for external factors.

caretakers, paying particular attention to added costs such as bonus payments and standby allowances.

– Oldham, for example, was able to achieve a substantial reduction in cost by reducing the standby cover for evenings and weekends from 29 staff to only four. This level was found to be adequate for the number of occasions when emergencies arose.

– Other authorities have changed the emphasis from caretakers assigned to individual blocks to a more general estate caretaking and cleaning service. Corby, for example, is making increasing use of door entry systems, to replace the traditional security role of caretakers, coupled with a mobile team of caretakers on cleaning and general estate upkeep duties. This combination has proved very popular with tenants and makes control and supervision more effective as well as providing substantial savings.

Services for the homeless and housing advice

47. Many authorities employ staff with specific duties in support of the homeless, in particular on homeless administration and in the staffing of hostels for the homeless. A number of authorities also have housing advice centres whose function can include advice to the homeless as well as to those seeking to purchase their council house and those requiring more general housing advice. Analysis shows that:

(a) Administration and welfare consumes 40% of total local authority expenditure on homelessness. This includes the cost of specialist staff engaged in dealing with domestic problems for homeless families (e.g. disputes, marital problems), co-ordination with Social Services and with other housing authorities, visiting, interviewing and assessing applications for accommodation from families who present themselves as homeless, as well as the cost of the necessary administrative and clerical support.

(b) Overall, hostels provide 40% of the temporary accommodation for the homeless and are the most important form of provision outside London. Not all authorities have hostels however; for those with such accommodation the figure is 70% overall. [The relative economics of hostels and bed and breakfast accommodation will be discussed in the next chapter.]

(c) Some 120 authorities have housing advice centres with specialist staff. In other authorities those functions are performed by the general administrative and other staff. Measuring the workload of these centres is made difficult by the definition of a case, since this can range from a short enquiry to a much more lengthy process.

48.   Table 6 below shows the variation in staffing levels for each of these activities within the different classes of housing authority. In each case, the difference between the lowest 25% (i.e. lowest quartile) authority and the highest 25% is a factor of at least 2 and in some cases as much as 4. That is, staffing per 1,000 housing advice cases in a quarter of metropolitan and shire districts is more than *four times* the figure in the quarter of authorities at the other end of the scale.

Table 6:   STAFFING AND SERVICES FOR THE HOMELESS AND HOUSING ADVICE, 1983–4
Full-time equivalents

	Shire Districts	Met. Districts	Outer London Boroughs	Inner London Boroughs
Homeless Administration staff per 1,000 applicants				
average	6.5	5.0	6.8	8.1
highest 25%	7.9	5.6	7.4	10.4
lowest 25%	2.9	2.2	3.8	4.7
Hostel staff per 10 units				
average	1.2	2.8	1.0	1.4
highest 25%	1.7	3.2	1.4	1.5
lowest 25%	0.5	1.2	0.3	0.7
Housing Advice staff per 1,000 cases				
average	2.7	2.0	1.5	3.1
highest 25%	3.3	2.1	1.6	5.0
lowest 25%	0.3	0.3	0.8	1.8

Auditors are now working with individual authorities to enable local management to be satisfied that higher-than-average staffing (where this is the case) is indeed reflected in higher service levels or justified by external conditions not covered in the detailed analysis. Any authority with staffing above the lowest 25% levels shown above should satisfy itself that there are good reasons to explain why it has been unable to match the levels achieved by many of the authorities listed in Appendix C.

Administrative support

49.   Some staff in housing management have been excluded from the analysis above. They are primarily concerned with administrative support and central management. Together these account on average for 21% of total staff. Table 7 illustrates the range of staffing numbers assigned to these tasks and emphasises the need for some authorities to review these particular overheads.

Table 7:   HOUSING ADMINISTRATION STAFF, 1983–4
Full-time equivalent staff per 10,000 dwellings

	Shire Districts	Met. Districts	Outer London Boroughs	Inner London Boroughs
Administrative support*				
Average	5.3	6.2	8.8	18.9
Highest 25%	13.5	12.1	23.4	32.2
Lowest 25%	4.9	5.5	6.7	13.9
Central management*				
Average	3.6	3.6	4.7	14.3
Highest 25%	10.1	8.4	12.2	22.3
Lowest 25%	3.1	2.9	3.9	10.9

* For definitions see below

Thus:

(a)   On average outside London there are six members of the *administrative support* staff (defined as covering all administration, clerical, typing and support services for the housing department plus staff dealing with supplies, accounts, personnel records, salaries, wages, etc.) for every 10,000 dwellings; but a quarter of all authorities have more than double this staffing level.

(b) Similarly for *central management* staff (defined as the senior or 'higher' management of the department, normally the first and second tier in the organisation, and housing staff requirements for the management of clearance and/or modernisation programmes). Outside London, there are four members of these management staff for every 10,000 dwellings on average; but 25% of authorities have almost three times this number of staff.

(c) An Inner London borough with (say) 40,000 dwellings within the highest quartile of authorities would have up to 100 more management staff than a metropolitan district of comparable size among the lowest quartile of metropolitan districts, in staffing terms. There is no evidence that the Commission has been able to collect to suggest that the higher staffing levels in London are reflected in better standards of service than are available in metropolitan authorities of comparable size and facing similar levels of urban deprivation.

* * *

50. Exhibit 6 showed the substantial range in staff working on supervision and management. Similar ranges in staffing levels are to be found in the various elements of the housing management function. Some of the variability is due to different external circumstances, to the nature of the stock, to the standard of service and indeed the organisation of the housing function. There are nonetheless many opportunities for more efficient staffing levels which authorities ought to examine. Substantial sums are at stake. The cost per dwelling of general supervision and management ranges from £80 to £120 per house for the middle 50% of authorities – every £10 represents about £50 million a year on a national scale. An internal examination of staffing levels is therefore a key ingredient of the steps to be taken by all parties concerned with this work, and this work is now under way at the local level.

51. In the meantime, Table 8 below suggests some general performance indicators which could be applied to determine whether detailed local investigation is warranted.

Table 8: PROPOSED HOUSING MANAGEMENT PERFORMANCE INDICATORS: ECONOMY
Full-time equivalents

	Benchmark	Cause for concern
Full-time equivalent staffing:		
– general supervision and management/1,000 dwellings	6.2	9.5
– waiting list admin/1,000 applicants	1.4	2.8
– rent collection/1,000 payments		
door to door	1.8	3.5
cash office	1.0	2.7
– rent accounting/1,000 new lets	2.8	6.6
– housing benefit admin/1,000 recipients	0.7	1.4
– homeless admin/1,000 applicants	3.0	7.9
– hostel staff/10 units	0.5	1.9
– housing advice/1,000 cases	0.4	2.7
– administrative support/10,000 dwellings	5.1	13.9
– central management/10,000 dwellings	3.1	10.3
– caretaking and cleaning/1,000 dwellings serviced	6.0	12.7

These are relatively crude, first level, performance indicators which will not necessarily adequately reflect local factors outside authorities' control. As described in Appendix B, the Commission has analysed the information provided in the Housing Questionnaire to provide (via auditors) every individual housing authority with a series of local performance indicators. These show, for all the measures in the table, the extent of any gap between local performance and 'good practice' already attained by authorities facing similar problems. Authorities and auditors are now working locally to agree the appropriate corrective action, if any.

STRENGTHENING TOP MANAGEMENT IN STRESS AREAS

52. In difficult situations, it is the quality of top management that is of decisive importance. The more difficult housing situations need the very best housing managers. However, there is disturbing evidence that management turnover in high stress areas is excessive and that it is becoming increasingly difficult to attract applicants of suitable quality; it is not uncommon to see these posts re-advertised. The responsibilities are not unimportant: a typical large authority might well have 40,000 dwellings and an annual rent roll of over £30 million a year. Directors of housing for major authorities currently command salaries of the order of £25–28,000 a year, with very few receiving over £30,000 a year.

53. There are three main reasons why it is apparently proving difficult to attract and keep senior managers in those situations where their talents are most needed:

(a) Salaries are not competitive with industry or with the housing associations. A recent survey by the Commission's study team revealed that typically a housing association pays up to £5,000 a year (plus other benefits) more than local authorities, for managing a comparable number of dwellings. And a local authority director of housing could expect to earn some £5–10,000 a year less than the managing director of an industrial concern with comparable revenues and payroll.

(b) Within the local authority housing field, the extra pay available in larger authorities is insufficient to compensate for the additional strain and hassle involved. For example, the well-regarded Director of Housing in an Inner London authority moved to a provincial city recently. In his new authority he has 14,600 fewer dwellings under his control, 9,000 fewer housing benefit cases, and 10,000 fewer tenants in arrears as well as a generally supportive council. His take-home pay following the move fell by under 10%. At the second tier level, the difference is under 5%.

(c) The level of political interference in day-to-day management of housing tends to be greatest in the areas of highest housing stress – partly, of course, because in such circumstances members feel particularly compelled to intervene, in an attempt to 'get something done'. The Commission has already made its views plain on the appropriate relationship between members and officers within local government, most recently in its evidence to the inquiry now being chaired by David Widdicombe QC: 'In many of the least well managed authorities facing the most difficult social and economic problems, members are seeking to set policy *and* manage services directly. This is the cult of the gifted amateur taken to dangerous extremes. It is as if councillors see their role as driving the buses as well as setting fare policies. And it inevitably sets up a vicious circle: officers with any ability and independence become frustrated and vote with their feet, leaving to join other authorities; services deteriorate, because the better officers have left; so members feel compelled to intervene in the management of the services; and even more officers leave. And so on'.

54.   The Commission has concluded that urgent consideration should be given to two practical sets of measures to deal with these difficult problems.

First, increased salaries should be paid to senior housing managers working in the particularly high stress authorities. The housing Z-scores provide a fairly reliable means of assessing housing deprivation, since they take account of such factors as the level of unemployment, overcrowding, lack of basic amenities (exclusive use of bath and inside WC), ethnic origins, single-parent families and pensioners living alone. Obviously, detailed consideration beyond the scope of this report will need to be given to the amount of any increase in management salaries, and to who should receive it – and indeed to the effect on other officers employed by the authority. However, an average increase of (say) £5,000 a year to five senior managers in each of the 30 housing authorities facing the most difficult problems would cost less than 0.2% of the total annual Urban Programme expenditure; it would represent an excellent investment if it served to persuade more high calibre managers to serve in the areas in question.

55.   Second, the professional independence and standing of chief housing officers needs to be strengthened, to enable them to withstand undue local political pressures. The Commission has already considered possible arrangements to secure this end in a local government context generally, in its evidence to the Widdicombe inquiry. In its written evidence to the inquiry the Commission made the following proposals, to ensure that the roles of members and officers are clearly distinguished one from the other:

(i)   Officers should be appointed to serve the council as a whole and their written advice should be generally available, to all members. Professional and managerial competence should be the sole selection criteria. Officers should be politically 'neutral' and ideological considerations should play no part whatsoever in their selection; they should be expected to give objective advice at all times.

(ii)   Appointment procedures for chief officers should be strengthened. With the objective of appointing the most competent people as chief officers, interview panels should be limited in size (normally to no more than five people) and should include at least one independent external assessor and members of the local opposition.

For all chief officer appointments, the assessors' ratification might be required, unless at least two apparently qualified candidates from outside the authority are interviewed by the panel (i.e. the assessor could have veto power over any internal appointments 'closed' to competition).

(iii)   Rolling three-year contracts renewable only by mutual consent should be considered for all chief officers, to safeguard both their professional independence and the position of members. The consent of the relevant Secretary of State, (e.g. the Secretary of State for the Environment in a case affecting a director of housing) should be required before any chief officer is dismissed in the middle of his or her contract. [The Controller of the Audit Commission is on a renewable three-year contract as it happens; and this appointment is subject to the approval of the Secretaries of State for the Environment and for Wales.]

The political and other pressures and sheer hassle to which senior managers in high stress areas are often subject make such arrangements particularly necessary in the housing context. Management must be free to manage, within overall policy directions established by members. In the Commission's view, attempts by elected members to do officers' jobs for them will lead – and have led – to poorer services.

* * *

This chapter has suggested steps to strengthen the management of housing services. In summary, members of local housing committees should be satisfied that overall management responsibility is clearly assigned to a single chief officer with a competent organisation, that communications with tenants are effective and services are adequately responsive to their needs, that staffing levels are in line with good practice – or justified by above-average services, and that senior managers are free to manage under their overall policy direction.

Unless management improves, the prospects for dealing promptly and effectively with the present unsatisfactory state of affairs are poor. However, better management is about more than economy. The next three chapters of this report recommend the further steps that the Commission believes are needed.

2. Providing better value

56.   At present, council house tenants tend to be poorer, and generally older than the overall population average. The following statistics illustrate the social challenge facing local housing authorities generally in England and Wales:

 - The median household income of council tenants (excluding old age pensioners, single parent families and the unemployed) is almost one-third lower than for owner-occupiers with a mortgage, according to information supplied by the DOE to the *Inquiry into British Housing* chaired by HRH the Duke of Edinburgh. The precise figures for 1982 were £7,419 against £10,787.
 - 57% of single parent families in England and Wales are council tenants, who account for less than one third of all households; in some estates, over half the tenants are single parents.
 - Over 62% of households in receipt of supplementary benefit in Great Britain are council tenants.
 - Around 40% of households with 6 or more persons live in council owned dwellings.

57.   In these circumstances, it is perhaps understandable that some housing managers have come to view tenants generally as potential problems, rather than as customers to be served as well as the available resources will allow. Perhaps unconsciously, in some areas a minimalist approach has been adopted: minimum rent for minimum services.

58.   Such an approach contains the seeds of many of the problems that now affect much of the stock of council housing. Design standards have emphasised quantity (i.e. density) and speed over quality, with all the problems associated with system building, tower blocks and deck access. Low rents have led to inadequate maintenance – since the funds are simply not there to keep buildings in reasonable condition. Inadequate maintenance itself leads to arrears, lengthy relet periods, and eventually to vandalism which in turn adds to costs and limits the scope for affordable service improvements.

59.   The Commission believes that rather than a minimalist approach, housing authorities should be seeking to provide better services and be prepared to charge more realistic rents for them – bearing in mind that housing benefit (now costing around £4.5 billion a year) exists to meet the bulk of housing costs of the more deprived families. Many housing authorities could take the following steps to upgrade the quality of the service they offer to their 'customers', which is how tenants should be viewed and treated:

  (i) Upgrade some of the more rundown estates, correcting the design mistakes of the past where possible.
 (ii) Minimise the number of empty properties.
(iii) Minimise the need to place homeless families in bed and breakfast accommodation.
 (iv) Provide improved support for the elderly, who will become an increasingly large proportion of council tenants in the future.

(v) Help to keep running costs for tenants down, in particular by helping them to conserve energy.

Each of these value improvement initiatives is described in more detail below.

LEARNING FROM PAST DESIGN MISTAKES

60.   Hindsight is almost invariably good, if not necessarily perfect. It is clear that serious design mistakes were made in the 1960s and early 1970s for which tenants and ratepayers are now having to pay. It is not simply a matter of structural defects and inadequate plumbing and heating, serious though these are. The high-rise, deck access, 'concrete jungle' estates have seemingly bred crime, vandalism and loneliness in many authorities – leading to the unedifying spectacle of a local authority seeking (unsuccessfully) to demolish a block of flats scarcely a decade old with a replacement value of perhaps £2 million.

61.   The experience of builders in renovating rundown inner-city property, of members of the Commission with experience of managing council housing as members or officers of housing authorities, and of academic researchers suggests some design principles for the future. These boil down to a few fairly basic messages: listen to what people want, rather than providing 'what they ought to want'; involve tenants in decisions affecting their homes and lives rather than relying on architects and planners who live somewhere else; design-in crime prevention rather than rely on detection after the event. In particular, housing authorities should be aware of the lessons to be drawn from the design mistakes of the past. In her book, *Utopia on Trial: Vision and Reality in Planning Housing**, Alice Coleman draws on a detailed examination of the relationships between different types of anti-social behaviour and the design characteristics of local housing.

62.   The Coleman study covered over 4,000 blocks of flats (containing over 100,000 dwellings and accommodating perhaps a quarter of a million tenants) and 4,000 houses; and revealed a close relationship between design problems (as measured by a count of the number of adverse design features) and crime, as Exhibit 8 shows. This led to recommendations to overcome some of the factors that tend to be associated with crimes: anonymity, lack of surveillance, and alternative escape routes. The Commission recognises that it must be for local housing authorities and their advisers to decide whether or not to apply particular design recommendations to specific schemes. But architects and planners should be required to justify apparently running additional risks with public funds. Specifically, the available research suggests that maintainability can be designed into schemes. So far as refurbishment of council *houses* is concerned, the following principles are worth bearing in mind:

(i)   There should be windows adequate for effective surveillance in front ground-floor living rooms.

(ii)   Front doors should not project forward to impede the line of sight from the windows, but should be recessed a little, so that if porches are added, they do not project either. Front-facing doors are better than sideways-facing. Glass panels in or beside the doors would assist surveillance.

(iii)   There should be no other projections from the facade which obstruct the view of the street from the windows, e.g. garages, meter compartments, pram sheds or dustbin kennels.

(iv)   The buffer zone in front of the house should be an individual garden and not a shared lawn. It should have waist-high walls

---

* Published in March 1985 by Hilary Shipman, ISBN 0-948096, price £7.95.

Exhibit 8

CRIME AND ADVERSE DESIGN FEATURES
(Percentage of blocks with each crime)
Sample: 729 blocks of flats in Southwark

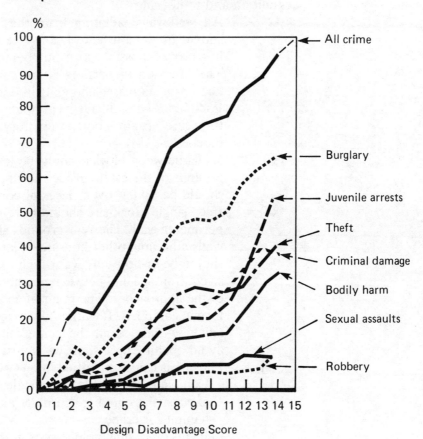

Source: <u>Utopia on Trial</u>, Coleman et al, May, 1985

and fences between neighbours and also along the street frontage, with gates. Low step-over fences that do not deter dogs, high faceless hedges or walls that impede surveillance and flimsy fencing materials should be avoided.

(v)   The minimum garden depth is 3 metres, but houses should not be set back much further than this if they are to have proper surveillance of the street approaches.

(vi)   Back gardens should be back-to-back without exits onto paths or roads. This design maximises security for toddlers, security against intruders and privacy. Access should be from the front, between detached or semi-detached houses, or through tunnels between pairs of terraced houses or through the garage. Tunnel access should begin inside the front gardens and not as an alleyway direct from the street. Layouts where the front of one row of houses faces the back of the next row are to be avoided.

(vii)   Each garage should be incorporated into the territory of the house where it is fully under its owner's control and less vulnerable to crime than in a segregated group of garages. The garage should not replace the main front window, making the house faceless.

(viii) Houses should be arranged in traditional streets, with all the open space allocated to individual front and back gardens.

35

Corner houses where the front garden swings round to face both roads, are preferable to end houses with their faceless side walls.

63. The following recommendations emerged from Coleman's research to improve living conditions for tenants of council *flats*, as an alternative to demolition and re-housing:

(ix) All walkways radiating from the block above ground level should be demolished or converted into private balconies as has proved possible in a number of refurbishment schemes. The insertion of barriers is not sufficient. Some blocks may need new staircases and exits in lieu of walkway access.

(x) Each block should have its grounds enclosed by a wall or fence to secure an autonomous territory, not shared by any other block.

(xi) Walls between blocks should be located to absorb the entire grounds of the estate inside the single-block territories. There should be no left-over pieces of confused space.

(xii) Each single-block site should have only one gate or gap in its perimeter wall. The rear grounds should be enclosed by high walls adjoining other housing or land uses. The front grounds should be enclosed by waist-high to chest-high walls along the street frontage and between neighbours, to permit surveillance of the approaches. The point of access should have a gate and formal gateposts. If traffic flow demands both an entrance and exit gate, these should be located on the same side of the site to avoid opening up a short cut across the grounds.

(xiii) Play areas can be modified in one of the following three ways:
  – Complete removal by sale or development; derelict land is expensive to hold and protect and all too often provides a habitat for crime.
  – Inclusion in single-block sites, if the residents wish it, so that they are restricted to fewer children who will then be less anonymous.
  – Enclosure in separate sites with independent entrances from the street, so that they no longer form part of the residential territory.

(xiv) Shops, services, clinics, nursery schools, estate offices, places of entertainment, etc., should be walled out of the residential territory.

(xv) After making each block autonomous in its own ground, attention should be paid to reducing its size. Lopping storeys off the top is a possibility in the following circumstances:
  – Where flats are in low demand, as in the north of England, storey lopping is being used to convert maisonettes into two-storeyed houses.
  – When roofs have to be replaced, it may be possible to reduce the height of the building at the same time. Some successful schemes involve 'top and tailing' four-storey blocks with flat roofs, converting them to two storeys and a pitched roof.
  – If a lift needs expensive replacement there may be a case for reducing the block walk-up height.
  – If a building is condemned to demolition, it may be feasible to save the bottom two storeys to convert to houses.

(xvi) The number of dwellings accessible on each floor should be as few as possible. The number of dwellings served by a single entrance should be reduced to 6–10. Ground floor flats can be given their own entrances and semi-private gardens, walled off from the communal entrances. Each block or self-contained section created by vertical or horizontal partitioning should be served by only one staircase.

(xvii) If the block is raised above ground level over stilts or garages, there is a case for inserting a few ground-floor flats located where the inhabitants can see the communal entrances. This helps to make the entrance less faceless.

(xviii) The entrance, or main entrance if there must be two, should face the street. In some cases this may be achieved by redesigning an estate road or path to incorporate the visual and functional characteristics of a public street.

(xix) Communal entrances should be equipped with a door instead of being merely a crude aperture, and the door should be glazed to make stairs and lifts visible from outside. As far as possible the communal entrances should be visible from at least some of the ground floor flats in the same blocks.

64.   These recommendations correspond closely with the conclusions of those members of the Commission with direct experience of the management and construction of council housing in inner-city areas. The experience of Westminster and Milton Keynes among other authorities confirms that general application of these recommendations will benefit both tenants and ratepayers. At minimum, *Utopia on Trial* should be read by all concerned with the management of local housing; and all housing authorities should submit all improvement schemes to careful evaluation in light of these well-researched recommendations.

MINIMISING THE NUMBER OF EMPTY PROPERTIES

65.   Approximately 2.4% of the current total housing stock of 4.8 million dwellings is vacant at any one time. At the end of March 1984, some 113,000 council owned dwellings were vacant, of which over 25,000 had been vacant for more than a year. Quite apart from the rent lost and likely damage from vandalism if property is empty, unnecessary delay in reletting properties reduces authorities' ability to provide for the homeless properly and increases the burden on local ratepayers. During the year ending March 1984, around 175,000 families presented themselves as homeless, of whom 75,000 were accepted as qualifying under the terms of the *Housing (Homeless Persons) Act* of 1977. In seven London boroughs, the number of families accepted as homeless was equivalent to over 50% of the total number of council dwellings let during the year. Exhibit 9 summarises the factors that need to be taken into account in making effective use of housing stock.

66.   The broad reasons why the 113,200 properties were empty were shown in the returns to the Department of Environment at end March 1984 and are set out in Table 9, together with the corresponding figures for the 26,100 of these dwellings which had been vacant for more than a year.

Table 9:   CLASSIFICATION OF VOIDS
March 31, 1984

	Total vacant	Vacant for more than 1 year
Available for letting	27,700	1,900
Undergoing repair or improvement	42,500	6,700
Awaiting repair or improvement	16,400	4,900
Other (including those awaiting sale or demolition)	26,600	12,600
	113,200	26,100

Exhibit 9

FACTORS INFLUENCING USE OF THE HOUSING STOCK

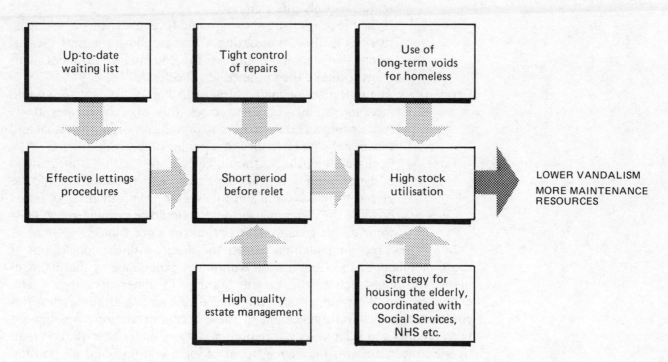

67.   Overall, local authorities' void rate of around 2.4% compares favourably with other sectors of the housing market. Recent evidence shows that for housing associations the void rate was 3.8%, for the private rented sector 4.2% and for government-owned property 6.9%*. Nonetheless, within the local authority sector there are many authorities which lie considerably above the average, and where significant improvements should be possible. Table 10 shows that there are wide variations between classes of authorities.

Table 10: BREAKDOWN OF VOID RATES
(Weighted average at March 31, 1984)
% dwellings

	Shire Districts	Met. Districts	Outer London Boroughs	Inner London Boroughs	Overall
	%	%	%	%	%
Available for letting	0.50	0.66	0.70	0.83	0.59
Undergoing repair or improvement	0.61	1.05	1.14	2.13	0.91
Awaiting repair or improvement	0.19	0.48	0.34	0.95	0.35
Other (including awaiting sale or demolition)	0.26	1.01	0.41	1.12	0.57
TOTAL	1.56	3.20	2.59	5.03	2.42

68.   The void rate is dependent on both the number of vacancies and the elapsed time taken to relet the property (the so-called relet period). The use of the void rate alone as an indicator would discriminate unfairly against authorities with high turnover and a large number of transfers. It is therefore the *relet period* that should be the focus of local authority management efforts. Considerable savings could be made if all authorities

* A recent Shelter report on the work of housing associations in inner cities indicates that in five large provincial housing authorities, voids among privately owned dwellings were 3.4%, compared with 3.3% for council owned dwellings.

could achieve the same average relet period as the more efficient. Analysis by the Commission's study team at a sample of authorities of different type and size revealed that the average relet period for normal management relets ranged from under two weeks in small shire districts up to six weeks in larger metropolitan and London authorities. In many authorities relet periods are considerably longer than this however.

69. Not all authorities can achieve the same relet period. Clearly the relet period is affected by policy decisions; for example in an authority that allows up to, say, three refusals per applicant the average relet period might be longer than if there were stricter rules. Further, different parts of the country may experience different problems – a property which would be highly desirable if in London may be relatively difficult to let in the north of England. And if a house is likely to be refused several times, more time spent on cleaning and redecoration may be worthwhile. However the figures shown above are evidently not unrealistic.

70. By following the good practices outlined in this chapter, at least a further 20,000 dwellings could become available for letting and expenditure on bed and breakfast could be reduced sharply – perhaps by more than £5 million. The experience of successful housing authorities suggests that minimising the relet period requires:

    (i) An efficient and fair system for administering the waiting list and allocating properties.

    (ii) Effective machinery for minimising the relet period.

These are discussed separately below.

Administering the waiting list

71. In total in England and Wales at the end of March 1984, there were 1.2 million applicants on local authority waiting lists. A further 600,000 tenants had applied for transfers to other council accommodation. New applicants to the waiting lists totalled over 500,000 during the year, each requiring to be processed for suitability and priority. In all, some 3,600 staff are directly involved in carrying out these activities.

72. These global figures perhaps mask the reality of the local situation. In a typical metropolitan district – which might have a stock of 35,000 dwellings – every week the housing department might relet 40 properties from the waiting list, rehouse 5 homeless families, execute 20 transfers and receive 100 new applications for council houses and 75 for transfers. Even though waiting lists can be manipulated to some extent, these statistics suggest at least two important conclusions:

    – Waiting lists are large and growing. In the above example, the figures imply an annual increase of 3,000 a year (in a list which might now stand at around 5,000) which would only partly be offset by natural wastage e.g. by applicants failing to renew their applications. In a typical Shire district, the figures can be even worse: 1,000 new applicants a year, an existing waiting list of 1,500 and 220 relets per year from the waiting list.

    – A large number of clients want to move from their existing accommodation for one reason or another. In a typical metropolitan district over 4,000 applications for transfer might be received during the year; however only a fraction of this number of transfers would take place. The comparable figures in a typical Shire district could be 700 and 80 respectively.

73. The figures also underline the importance of fair and efficient administration of waiting lists. The administration of the waiting list is an integral part of the allocation process and thus has a direct bearing on the effective use of the housing stock. A well managed list that is kept up to date and easily accessible can contribute to shorter relet periods and to the future well-being of the prospective tenant.

74. The task is far from simple. Waiting list details of prospective tenants (i.e. those likely to be housed within the next year, say) need to be kept up to date so that correct allocation decisions are made and relet periods minimised. Applications should be reviewed at least biennially and ideally annually to ensure that the list does not contain names of applicants who no longer require housing (moved away, died, etc.).

- Some authorities put the onus for renewal of an application onto the applicant – local advertisements invite existing applicants to reapply. This is cost effective but may distort the picture, for example, where applicants do not see the advertisement.
- Other authorities send out a letter or card requiring applicants to confirm that they are still interested in council accommodation and to notify any changes in circumstances. This is often done once a year, for the whole list.
- The most effective method is to produce renewal reminders automatically on the anniversary of the date of application. This 'rolling renewal' has the advantage of spreading the workload throughout the year. This is easier if the waiting list is computerised.

75. Authorities should try to strike a balance between the effort involved in a renewal of the complete list and the possibility of relet delays occurring as a result of an out-of-date list. In some circumstances, a complete renewal may be unproductive if, for example, those near the bottom of the list are unlikely to be housed for a considerable time. Some authorities have a policy of checking the details only for those applicants with a realistic expectation of an offer within the following year (e.g. perhaps only the top 10% of the general waiting list).

76. Allocations are made from the list usually according to locally defined rules about priorities. A system is needed to match the stock with the applicants' requirements, in order to enable fast allocation decisions to be made and to minimise the number of refusals, which add to the relet period. In most cases systems are designed to reflect the assessed degree of need of the prospective tenant (e.g. medical reasons, physical disability, social factors). Most systems can be operated effectively; and any explicit system is better than an informal allocation system which could be criticised as allowing irrelevant factors (e.g. race, political allegiance, personal links with council officers or members) to influence letting decisions.

77. Local authorities recognise that a points system can have perverse effects, particularly in areas where waiting lists are long. For example some authorities give priority to pregnant women; and members of authorities regularly cite instances where young women seek to jump the housing queue by deliberately becoming single parents. In this way, some local housing policies might have had the effect of increasing the number of single-parent families which is already disturbingly high. In some authorities up to 50% of live births are to unmarried mothers, may of whom are very young. Similarly, policies with regard to housing problem families affect the condition of council estates: tenants often ascribe the deterioration of their estate to the introduction of a relatively few problem families. Housing authorities are thus often placed in a 'no win' situation, having to decide between social and housing policy considerations. It is clearly impossible to suggest any general good practice guidelines – although there is general agreement that it makes sense to avoid accommodating problem families in high-rise flats where good neighbourliness is of special importance.

78. Policies on refusals can clearly have an important effect both on the time to relet and on the eventual tenant mix. There is a tendency for those

in more desperate housing need to become concentrated in the less popular estates, which other applicants already more comfortably housed may refuse in the expectation of a better offer later. This aspect has been covered in other research, notably a Working Paper No. 12: *Housing Policy and the Inner City*, from the School of Advanced Urban Studies (SAUS) of the University of Bristol.

Minimising the relet period   79.   Reductions to the relet period are possible not only by speeding the letting process but also by reductions to the waiting time for repair and improvement and indeed the length of time taken for these tasks. Better co-ordination could also ensure that lettings staff are able to act on reliable future completion dates. The figures shown in Exhibit 10 are estimates of

Exhibit 10

RELET PERIODS, FY 1984

All relets, weeks

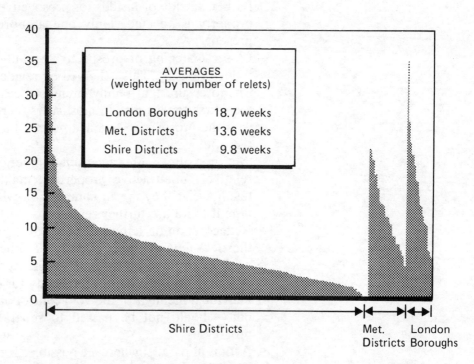

Source: Audit Commission Survey, 1985

the relet period based on the average void rate and the annual number of relets in each authority*. They relate to all vacant dwellings (including those requiring maintenance and improvement). The overall weighted average is 11 weeks but there is wide variation by type of authority – from 10 weeks for Shire districts to over four months in Inner London. Clearly a property requiring extensive maintenance will have a longer relet period than a normal management relet; but measures to speed the eventual relet are equally applicable, and some authorities modernise and/or refurbish with the tenant still in occupation. If the current national average relet period were to be reduced by 2½ weeks (which should be readily achievable by comparing the performance of the best 25% of authorities of all types with the rest) an additional 20,000 dwellings would be made available for

---

* The chart shows the average relet period for every housing authority. Thus in the worst London borough, for instance, the period was over 30 weeks and in the best, 7 weeks. A leading US property company with a stock of over 60,000 dwellings for rent aims for a void interval of 5 *days* – even where major improvements are required.

occupation. Assuming a weekly rent of £15, this is equivalent to additional income of over £15 million a year in addition to the extra rate income to the authority. The equivalent cost of an increase in the total housing stock of this size (i.e. by new build) would be over £500 million.

80.   A number of measures taken by the more efficient authorities to reduce the relet period and hence void levels are worthy of more general application:

- Enforcement of tenancy agreements where possible covering such matters as: four weeks notice of vacancy; maintenance of property in good decorative condition; tenant responsibility for minor repairs.
- Inspection of property as soon as notice received so that any essential work can be timetabled into the repairs staff work programme. (Although this practice necessitates double inspections it can still be cost-effective in speeding up the relet).
- Pre-allocation to a prospective tenant – a practice followed by about half of authorities – and encouragement of pre-viewing (either outside or inside) for prospective tenants, i.e. before the property is vacated. Only one authority in four does this at present.
- Closer matching of prospective tenant to property in order to reduce refusals. This is helped by regular renewal of the waiting list, to ensure that family circumstances have not changed since their first application. In most cases there should be an interview with the prospective tenant to check the position and to explain the offer.
- 'Multiple offers' after a certain number of refusals (say three) for relatively unattractive properties, making clear to prospective tenants that they are in competition with others. This can save time if there are further refusals.
- Redecoration on letting (if necessary) to be the responsibility of the new tenant (unless elderly or otherwise unable to do the work) with financial or other assistance from the authority.
- Assignment of overall responsibility for each void property to an individual member of the void control or lettings staff. Responsibility should not be passed to separate sections as the relet progresses.
- Action in parallel wherever possible. If repairs work is necessary then this should be co-ordinated by voids control staff, and carried out with tenant *in situ* if at all possible [For this to be a credible policy without increasing refusal rates, repairs must be undertaken promptly]. Usually only repairs for 'health and safety' reasons and essential cleaning should be done while the property is empty.
- Tight control of work by the DLO or contractors; 'progress chasing' by voids control staff, with penalty clauses for failure to meet target repair dates; health and safety checks and minor repairs to enable rapid relet should have priority.
- Letting properties on the basis of forecast repair dates, so that the new tenant can move in as soon as the repairs are complete. Such a policy would necessitate a marked improvement in performance of many DLOs and contractors where repair completion dates are at present unreliable.
- Regular monitoring of the void position; reports to committee listing properties vacant for more than one month, and the average relet period broken down by area; setting of targets against which monitoring reports can be compared.

81.   Special initiatives are required for 'difficult to let' properties if the position is not to deteriorate still further. Where resources for substantial improvement or refurbishment are not immediately available, other measures have been found to be effective:

- Improved security, perhaps for individual blocks, by employing security staff and/or installing entryphones. In one authority the initiative came from the existing tenants and the scheme is self-financing – the tenants were willing to pay a service charge of £3 per week. This illustrates a rather different aspect of void control – not only are the properties more attractive to prospective tenants, but the existing tenants are more likely to stay, thus reducing the turnover rate.

- Agreements with other bodies to take over the management of estates or blocks including responsibility for allocations, tenancy conditions and minor repairs. For example, some authorities have reached agreement for this with local universities and training colleges.

- Advertising in the local press to anyone on the existing waiting list, regardless of priority. This is a more general case of the 'multiple offer' mentioned above, and may be attractive to those likely to have a long wait otherwise. Advertising in the local press to the general public can also produce useful results. In some authorities this has revealed a large latent demand for council accommodation from people who have been otherwise deterred from applying, perhaps by residency rules. In one Inner London borough tenants were found for 500 void dwellings during one weekend in this way.

- Short-term lets to transient workers, job seekers or students. Consideration could be given to converting some blocks into homeless hostels or single persons' accommodation (of which there is a considerable shortage).

- Particular efforts to 'sell' less desirable properties to prospective tenants, perhaps by the use of accompanied visits and/or lower rents. An explanation of the attractive features of a property (e.g. future plans for estate improvement) might outweigh some of the perceived disadvantages, particularly if coupled with advice that the alternative to the property on offer might be a considerable wait (for non-priority applicants) until a more attractive property becomes available.

82.   These initiatives can be taken by an authority acting on its own. (Possible vehicles for joint public/private sector investment in low cost housing for rent are discussed in Chapter 4.) But not all of the above procedures are feasible in every situation. Some properties are left in such a poor state of repair as to require major works before they can be offered for letting. Many incoming tenants are single parent families, some of whom may not be able to redecorate their property, even with financial assistance. Many authorities experience problems of 'moonlight flits' where the tenant gives no notice at all. In certain areas, officers find it difficult to achieve more than a week's notice and hence cannot normally operate pre-allocation and previewing policies. Even when these are carried out there may be a higher refusal rate if previously hidden defects come to light only when the property is vacated. Further delays may occur if the prospective tenant is waiting for a one-off furniture allowance from DHSS (although these should in theory be made very quickly – most authorities overcome this problem by keeping a store of spare furniture in order to provide the basic minimum to enable a home to be occupied immediately, particularly

Exhibit 11

MODEL LETTING PROCEDURE

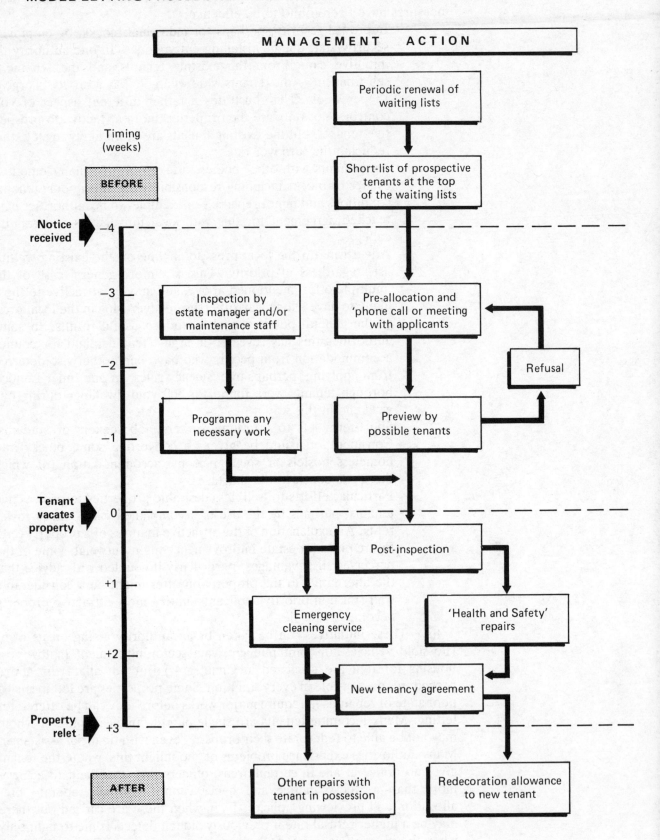

44

for relets to homeless families). Problems such as these, and possible solutions to them are discussed in a report recently produced by the Institute of Housing*. The DOE circular *Local Authority Empty Dwellings* (12/85) also sets out a range of methods of controlling voids.

83. Whatever the extent of local problems, the key to minimising the relet period is effective co-ordination of council effort, to bring together the several activities required for rapid relet of a vacated property. An individual member of a separate voids control section within the housing department should be assigned responsibility for reletting each property within the target period. A procedure to achieve rapid relets is illustrated in Exhibit 11. Authorities ought to set a target to relet those dwellings not subject to major repairs and improvement within three weeks. Only properties awaiting major repair and improvements or demolition should be exempt from this target and even some of these properties may be suitable as temporary accommodation for homeless families. At least one authority manages to achieve a turnaround in a matter of days, sometimes a same-day transfer in certain circumstances. This is, after all, the accepted practice in the owner-occupied sector.

84. The members' role in void control should be to set and monitor overall targets and performances. There are many examples of reports to committee, with summary statistics of relets during each period and, importantly, listing properties vacant for more than a given length of time (typically 3 months, although this is probably too long to ensure control over ordinary lets – one month would be more effective). However, in the Commission's view, members should not become involved in the allocation process itself. In one authority visited by the study team every allocation decision is passed to the appropriate local member for his comment or approval. No matter how conscientious and hard-working the individual members are, this inevitably increases the relet period; and it can lay members open to accusations e.g. of racial bias and favouritism, however unjustifiably. This view of the members' role was set out as long ago as 1969 [in *Council Housing Purposes, Procedures and Priorities, HMSO*].

HOUSING THE HOMELESS

85. An aspect of housing management related to both allocations and void control is an authority's statutory duties in administering the *Housing (Homeless Persons) Act* of 1977. This is a difficult area for many councils where homeless applicants are competing for the allocation of vacant dwellings with applicants on the normal waiting list. Exhibit 12 shows the number of families accepted as homeless in relation to each authority's relets during 1983–84.

86. Of course not all homeless families were allocated to permanent tenancies; but the scale of the problem is indicative:
  – In 1983–84, as mentioned above, around 175,000 households presented themselves as homeless, under half of which were accepted as qualifying and in need of accommodation according to the criteria of the Act (this figure includes those rehoused directly).
  – The problem is concentrated on the larger metropolitan authorities and particularly in London – the number of families occupying bed and breakfast accommodation in London has almost tripled over the last three years, to almost 3,000 families at the end of 1984. For example, in two Inner London boroughs, for every 100 relets there were nearly 70 families accepted as homeless.

---

* *The Key to Empty Housing* (IOH, December 1985)

Exhibit 12

HOMELESS FAMILIES AND AVAILABLE COUNCIL DWELLINGS, FY 1984

Ratio of families accepted as homeless to total relets in year

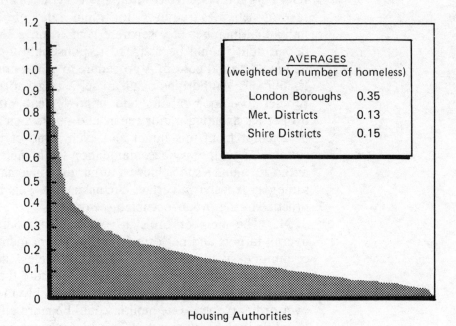

Source: Audit Commission Survey, 1985

- A high proportion of all families presenting to local authority homeless family units are single-parent families. A recent survey suggests that almost 45% of all homeless families in London are single-parent families and that one in seven has a head of household under 21.
- The total cost of homelessness to local authorities was £28.6 million (net) in 1983–84 and rose to over £34 million in 1984–85. This increase can be compared to the increase in DHSS' cost of supplementary benefit board and lodging payments, which have risen from £76 million in 1980 to an estimated £380 million in 1984.

Table 11, drawn from analysis of information in a recent Shelter report, *A Decent Home Makes all the Difference* shows the position in four large cities. It indicates that there are as many empty dwellings as there are homeless families; it also demonstrates that there are often more empty privately owned dwellings than voids for which the council might be held responsible.

Table 11: HOMELESSNESS AND VOIDS IN FOUR PROVINCIAL CITIES, 1984

	Families accepted as homeless	Empty dwellings Private	Council-owned
Birmingham	5,045	5,600	3,700
Leeds	1,605	5,900	2,700
Liverpool	930	4,900	3,400
Nottingham	1,000	3,600	1,400
	8,580	20,000	11,200

87.   In fact, very few councils house a significant proportion of homeless families directly into a council dwelling. A discussion of ways to prevent homelessness (and the increase in single-parent families which is an important contributory cause) and of the appropriate scale for the nation's house-building programme is beyond the scope of this report. In any case, any policy changes will take time to be reflected in improvements on the ground. In the real world, there are usually three options for housing the homeless open to authorities: purpose built (or adapted) hostels, bed and breakfast, and hard-to-let or short life property. Analysis of the available data shows that bed and breakfast is usually the most expensive option, even though almost 60% of housing authorities make regular use of this accommodation – over 900,000 bed/nights are likely to be involved this year. The average gross cost of a night's bed and breakfast accommodation for a family is about £19 a night as Table 12 shows – above the average *weekly* rent in most council dwellings.

Table 12:   BED AND BREAKFAST ACCOMMODATION FOR THE HOMELESS, 1983–4

	% of authorities using B & B	No. of nights (thousands)	Average cost per night per family
	%		(£)
Shire Districts	60	201	17
Metropolitan Districts	30	11	29
Outer London	74	327	16
Inner London	75	303	23
All Authorities	58	842	19

The variation about the average however is very large – authorities of a similar type paying between £4.00 and nearly £50.00 a night per family. This variation may in part reflect differences in the quality of the accommodation provided and the lead-time given to the landlord – late and individual bookings are likely to be more expensive.

88.   Hostels are generally better places to accommodate homeless families than bed and breakfast. Hostels have some degree of supervision and security, rather than bed and breakfast which may have to be vacated during the day. Hostels usually provide a better standard of accommodation and for authorities with hostel accommodation, the average cost per family night can be much lower than for bed and breakfast accommodation. It is often difficult to establish the true cost of running a hostel, but a typical cost (including capital costs but not central overheads) is of the order of £12 a night per hostel unit, compared with the figure above of £19 per family a night in bed and breakfast (the cost is now often over £30 in London). On the basis of these figures investment in additional hostel accommodation would probably provide attractive returns for authorities with a high baseload of bed and breakfast use.

89.   Clearly where hostels exist it is important to use them fully. Surprisingly, in some authorities the average hostel utilisation over the year was lower than 50% and yet significant amounts were spent on bed and breakfast. When a hostel place becomes vacant, a review of those in bed and breakfast should be carried out with the intention of filling the hostel place as soon as possible rather than keeping it empty until the next homeless family appears. Of those authorities using both bed and breakfast and hostels, two thirds have hostel occupancy rates of less than 80%.

90.   A number of initiatives are worth considering to reduce the costs of providing accommodation for the homeless in the short term, i.e. until additional hostel accommodation can be provided:
   – Some authorities have reduced their average costs by 'block

booking' sufficient accommodation to cope with the underlying local level of homelessness on a longer term basis.

- Authorities often accumulate empty dwellings in a block of flats awaiting improvement. It is important that those responsible for the provision of accommodation for the homeless should work closely with void control staff to take up these opportunities.
- One local group of Shelter drew attention to a number of empty Ministry of Defence properties in the area, many of which had been vacant for several years. The local authority is exploring ways in which these properties could be used to house the large number of families currently in local bed and breakfast accommodation.
- Other initiatives to alleviate the shortage of accommodation for the homeless include schemes whereby the local authority temporarily leases private sector accommodation, taking on the management responsibility and guaranteeing that the property will be vacated by a specified date.

IMPROVING HOUSING SERVICES FOR THE ELDERLY

91. About one quarter of the dwellings built recently by local authorities have been sheltered housing; and direct expenditure by housing authorities on services for the elderly is estimated to total almost £95 million (gross) in 1983–84. This does not include debt charges, maintenance costs or an apportionment of general supervision and management expenditure, but does include the cost of warden services and the normally hidden charges such as deficits on central heating and the cost of other items such as community centres at sheltered schemes, communal lighting and gardening. There are over 350,000 local authority sheltered and other dwellings providing some sort of warden service to the elderly. Some of the more common services for the elderly are:

(a) **Purpose-built sheltered accommodation,** often with warden services and enhanced facilities e.g. alarms in every room. Sheltered schemes are a means of keeping the elderly in the community as long as possible. The warden provides occasional help for the residents and is on hand in the event of emergencies (e.g. a fall or inability to get out of bed). Wardens cannot replace the social services or NHS; their role is to organise rather than provide care.

(b) **'Very sheltered'** accommodation, known as 'Part 2½' Schemes. Their objective is to provide additional care and facilities to permit elderly people to remain even longer in the community and to avoid them becoming residents of the homes run by Social Services' departments which provide for the chronically infirm, disabled or senile elderly.

(c) **Sheltered and very sheltered accommodation** on a single integrated site with common support facilities. The objective is to avoid the disruptive effects of moving people to different schemes, as their dependency increases with age. People become attached to their home, their friends and their surroundings and find it distressing to move even when increased disability makes other accommodation more suitable.

(d) **Central alarm systems.** These provide a simple electronic means of alerting the warden. Newer systems enable a tenant to open a two-way speech channel by depressing a portable alarm switch. With such systems, a call for help can be answered by deploying a mobile warden, police, fire or other forms of assistance. A central alarm system has many advantages:
- Giving tenants immediate access to help 24 hours a day, and the sense of security that this provides.

- Enabling warden staff to enjoy their leisure time because they can switch over to the central system when they go off duty.
- Achieving economies in relief warden staff in some cases.
- Connecting elderly private sector residents to a support facility.
- Providing an alternative to sheltered accommodation for the less dependent.

Some schemes provide alarm station staff with access via video screens to computer systems which maintain tenants' records and the frequency of visits. Such systems can also contain a list of tenants' disabilities and be used to calculate wardens' workload.

(e) **Mobile Wardens.** A few authorities provide a service whereby wardens visit tenants in their homes, usually in accordance with a fixed visiting plan. Such services were mostly introduced before new technology provided reliable central alarm systems.

Table 13 shows the number of dwellings providing special services for old people, broken down by class of authority. This represents less than 8% of the stock; yet an estimated 15% of council tenants are aged over 75 now; and the number of elderly tenants is likely to increase by 30–40% in the next decade.

Table 13: DWELLINGS WITH SERVICES FOR THE ELDERLY, 1983–4
('000)

	Shire Districts	Met. Districts	Outer London Boroughs	Inner London Boroughs
Category 1 & 2 sheltered dwellings	174	59	15	7
Part 2½ (very sheltered) dwellings	2	2	*	0
Central alarm linked dwellings (with no resident warden)	36	12	*	1
Mobile warden service (no alarm)	27	20	2	3
TOTAL	239	93	17	11
% of total stock	9.5	6.4	4.7	3.0

* Very Small

92. The cost of providing support for the elderly residents varies widely, both by type of dwelling and by type of authority, as Table 14 indicates.

Table 14: INCREMENTAL ANNUAL REVENUE COST OF SERVICES FOR THE ELDERLY, 1983–4
£ per dwelling

	Shire Districts	Met. Districts	Outer London Boroughs	Inner London Boroughs	F.t.e. staff per 100 dwellings
Mobile warden service (no alarm)	60	50	75	85	0.5–1.5
Central alarm (without resident warden)	180	150	NA	NA	0.5–2*
Supervised sheltered dwellings	320	270	390	430	3–6
All types	270	210	355	330	

NA Insufficient data
* Includes control room staff (24-hour cover) and the mobile wardens providing emergency cover.

The costs shown *exclude* additional debt charges, maintenance and any apportionment of general supervision and management expenditure on sheltered accommodation compared with 'normal' council housing stock – these could easily add £300–400 a year to the cost of supervised sheltered accommodation. Very few London boroughs operate central alarm systems so there is insufficient data to determine an average. For the other authorities the figures shown above almost certainly overstate the cost of central alarms. The survey data will include relatively large set-up costs for these systems – the marginal cost per dwelling of additional connections is only a fraction of the average costs shown, possibly as low as £100 per dwelling. 'Supervised sheltered' dwellings (i.e. all those with resident wardens) are considerably more expensive. Since there are very few part $2\frac{1}{2}$ dwellings nationally it has not been possible to determine a separate cost figure although these will plainly be more expensive because of the 24-hour warden cover and the higher service level generally.

93. The Commission published a report a year ago on care of the elderly by Social Services' departments: *Managing Social Services for the Elderly More Effectively*. This drew attention to the need for better co-ordination between housing and social services departments. The problem is especially serious in Shire districts where housing and social services are under the control of separate authorities. The key problem is to ensure that the level of care and support provided to elderly tenants is appropriate to their needs. The evidence available to the Commission suggests that this is often not the case, and that large amounts of resources could be better targeted. This is an area of some debate in the housing and social services professions: it is argued, for example, that a mix of tenants can provide a degree of 'good neighbour' self-help and thus relieve pressure on a resident warden. It is also felt by some professionals that too high a level of personal support to relatively able elderly tenants can in fact lead to a higher level of dependency. This has an important bearing on service levels and the definitions of wardens' duties. However, it is evident that demand for purpose-built sheltered accommodation is always likely to outstrip supply; and the high level of satisfaction among tenants in sheltered housing must be balanced against the large number of disappointed applicants, many of them continuing to live in homes which they own but cannot afford to maintain properly. This emphasises the need for the limited resources available to be distributed as fairly as possible.

94. Fortunately, recent advances in technology have changed the balance of care options that are available to those who are not dependent on a high level of service.* The dependency of clients enjoying central alarm, mobile wardens and conventional sheltered housing are often very similar. Councils must therefore compare the incremental cost against the benefits of other methods. From the figures in Table 14 above, equipping tenants' existing accommodation with a link to a central alarm station can be very much more cost effective than transferring an elderly person with only minor disabilities into more sheltered accommodation in order to provide assistance on the few occasions when this may be needed. [The same benefits could be provided by housing authorities for owner-occupiers, many of whom may eventually require Social Services' support. Central Government should ensure that authorities have the statutory powers to provide this service]. Moreover, alarm systems built in to the existing telephone network can prove less obtrusive than other types of alarm which some tenants regard as signalling a state of dependency that they neither feel nor welcome.

One authority visited by the study team, Langbaurgh, has taken full advantage of the benefits of new technology, and is now fully committed to the use of central alarm systems for its elderly tenants. The system now provides more widespread cover, at a lower cost, than was originally provided by resident wardens:

- In 1982–83 the authority spent close to £500,000 providing warden services at 3,000 category 1 and 2 dwellings.

---

*See for example *Staying at Home – Helping Elderly People* by A. Tinker (HMSO: 1984)

- Projected increases in cost led to a decision to convert all these dwellings to a central alarm system. Staffing of 78 wardens (plus 57 reliefs) has been reduced (using a policy of no redundancy and redeployment) to less than 20 full-time equivalent staff.
- The control station is staffed 24 hours a day and mobile wardens can respond rapidly to an emergency anywhere in the area. For a capital investment of less than £800,000, revenue expenditure has been reduced to half that in 1982–83.
- For a further investment of £250,000, alarms have been fitted in all general council accommodation where requested by elderly or handicapped tenants, and the service is being offered to local housing associations, county social services and the district health authority.

95.   The solution described above may not provide the mix of housing services required by some authorities (for social, policy or other reasons). But there would be substantial savings nationally if only a fraction of the elderly currently receiving a premium warden service were to be provided with a service more appropriate to their needs. The potential value improvement by this means is at least £40 million a year. This is not to imply that existing elderly tenants should be moved to other accommodation if unwilling to do so. But the number of people aged 85 and over is expected to rise by 35% between 1984 and 1996, and it is important that authorities decide their policies now for providing housing services for these potential clients.

96.   Where more expensive sheltered facilities are provided, authorities should ensure that as far as possible the rent payable reflects the extra cost of the services. Often tenants of sheltered accommodation with a warden service are charged only a nominal £1 a week and some make no additional payments at all. The average charge is only £3 per week which clearly does not cover the additional costs of services for the elderly shown in Table 14. At present, many elderly tenants are in receipt of full housing benefit (up to 80% in some authorities) and there is perhaps a case for a greater share of the extra costs to be met by the tenant (and via housing benefit), not by other council tenants or by ratepayers – although it would be premature to make any changes until the future shape of housing benefit is clarified.

97.   Physical security is a particular concern for the elderly. Much can be done to overcome the fear of crime among old people by the encouragement of ideas such as the Neighbourhood Watch scheme and community policing, which are relatively simple to implement. Hammersmith and Fulham, for instance, has recently taken the initiative in distributing to residents a crime prevention handbook and in holding local exhibitions to promote greater awareness of the steps that can be taken to prevent crime locally. Consideration of tenant security is also important in maintenance and improvement programmes, and in arrangements for caretaking and other services (e.g. entryphone systems). In the longer term, the design and construction of estates should reflect the growing concerns about crime prevention and the lessons summarised earlier in this chapter. The Home Office Standing Conference on Crime Prevention has issued a report* on residential burglary, which covers ideas such as these.

MINIMISING TENANTS' FUEL BILLS

98.   One useful service that authorities can provide is to ensure that tenants' energy bills are as low as possible – not least because heating costs can easily amount to over 40% of rents and can thus contribute to arrears problems if they are unduly high.

---

* *Report of the Working Group on Residential Burglary:* (Home Office, November 1985).

99. The most obvious step is to ensure that when property is modernised, the opportunity is taken to install insulation and draught-proofing, ensure that the heating system is efficient and that thermostats control temperature in the main living rooms. Some authorities have undertaken partial modernisation, omitting some obvious energy-saving measures in order to make the available resources stretch a little further. This may be attractive politics, in a sense that something is done to more homes, but it is not sound economics in the long run.

100. Many authorities are considering abandoning district heating schemes which do not, generally, enjoy a good reputation. About 350,000 council dwellings (7%) are heated by means of group or district heating schemes. Such schemes typically service 100–300 dwellings, although group heating in sheltered schemes may cover only 20–30 dwellings; and at the other extreme up to 5,000 dwellings can be served from a single boiler plant. Experts in this field have advised the Commission that local authority performance varies considerably and is often deficient, particularly in two respects:

(a) As in many other areas the information available to management is inadequate. The charges for the maintenance and servicing of district heating schemes are often not separated from general housing maintenance charges. The housing manager, in the role of client, has no method of monitoring the value for money that is being obtained.

(b) The efficiency of the district heating schemes themselves is highly variable. Consumption per dwelling ranges from 500 to 1200 therms per annum (although this is obviously also a function of factors such as dwelling size and the degree of insulation).

101. In the past the viability of a district heating scheme has depended not so much on the relative price of the heat source, but on the density of dwellings serviced and hence the costs of the associated pipework. More recently, however, lower cost mains systems have become available and potential new district heating schemes ought to be appraised in this light. In any event, authorities should consider the opportunities for refurbishment of existing systems. Considerable improvements can be made, particularly in medium size and multi-storey developments which are presently heated by electricity or oil and where the option of individual gas heating is not available. Recent advances in control technology and in insulation standards can bring useful benefits.

Methods to improve efficiency include the following:

(a) Investigation of existing heat service supply agreements. These often relate to 'anticipated' rather than 'actual' energy consumption.

(b) The use of high efficiency electronic heat meters in boilerhouses. This is becoming more widespread since heat is purchased by the authority 'at the boilerhouse wall'; inadequacies in operational boiler plant efficiencies are then not reflected in increased charges to the customer.

(c) Fitting a water meter on the supply to central boiler plants, to detect losses from undergound mains which can result in 'hidden' charges to the customer.

(d) Installing effective consumer controls. These generally comprise electrically operated valves to shut off heating and hot water supply under the control of a programmer operated by the tenant, together with, in some instances, installation of individual electronic heat meters and pre-payment heat controllers. These and other aspects should be considered with a view to reducing consumption and hence cost.

102. There is considerable disparity in the approaches adopted by authorities with regard to methods of assessing charges to tenants. Some use flat rate charges; some still utilise evaporative meters and some a mixture of both. Several local authorities are now employing electronic heat meters and pre-payment heat controllers. [Evaporative meters only measure the heat from the radiator and not the pipework which can continue to emit uncharged heat all the year round. Where single pipe loop systems are in use, 50% of the heat supplied can remain unmetered, thus producing deficits on district heating operating accounts.]

103. Before deciding to replace district heating a detailed assessment of the consequential costs which will be incurred by the authority in addition to the costs for the replacement gas/solid fuel systems should be carried out. This should include the costs for: electricity supply reinforcement, redecoration/disturbance allowances, terminating existing heat service agreements, modifying boiler plant and pump outputs during conversion, preparing contract documents and professional fees, together with cost of local authority officers' time. The costs for maintaining the replacement heating equipment in individual dwellings should also be included – this is often not identified explicitly in later maintenance programmes.

* * *

This chapter has suggested some ways in which services to housing authorities' customers could be improved. Maintenance – arguably one of the most important services, and certainly a source of a considerable volume of complaints – is covered in a separate Commission report to be published later in 1986. Table 15 summarises some general, first level indicators of the effectiveness of the local housing service, which are consistent with those suggested in Table 8 for evaluating the economy of the local service. As with the economy indicators included at the end of Chapter 1, more detailed performance appraisals on void control have been given to all authorities, via their auditors.

Table 15: PROPOSED HOUSING MANAGEMENT PERFORMANCE INDICATORS: EFFECTIVENESS

	Benchmark	Cause for Concern
Capital Schemes on new build and refurbishment: design lessons applied		
– Houses (para 62)	5 out of 8	3 out of 8
– Flats (para 63)	7 out of 11	5 out of 11
Average relet period (normal relets)		
– London	6 weeks	12 weeks
– Provinces	3 weeks	6 weeks
Homeless families		
– Hostel occupancy (if bed and breakfast also used)	>80%	<50%
– Average time in bed and breakfast	4 weeks	8 weeks
Central alarm links per 1,000 elderly tenants provided with warden services	500	200
Average group or district heating cost per dwelling	£200/year	£400

However, all services must be paid for eventually by the tenant, ratepayer or taxpayer (e.g. via housing benefit and rate support grant). Wherever the funds come from, housing authorities need sound financial management to ensure that their income is received on time and expenditure is under control. This is the subject of the next chapter of this report.

3. Tighter financial control

104. The total rent roll of local housing authorities in England and Wales amounts to some £3.6 billion a year – average rent of around £15 a week for 4.8 million dwellings. Of this, in many authorities over half is met by the taxpayer in form of housing benefit, with the balance being paid by tenants (who also pay rates, of course) and ratepayers when there is a deficit on the Housing Revenue Account (HRA).

105. Obviously, it is important to tenants and ratepayers alike that sums of this order of magnitude are under tight and effective control. This is not always the case. For example, in one Inner London borough, the local auditor has observed serious problems:

- Rent levels have not been reviewed in the past four years; so rent for a 2-bedroom dwelling within a 20 minute journey of the City of London is now some £3 a week below the Inner London average and over £5 a week lower than in Middlesbrough (for example).
- Average maintenance expenditure is less than half the level needed to keep the stock in reasonable repair; and there is a very considerable capital maintenance backlog.
- Notwithstanding the low rent and the fact that over 65% of tenants receive some form of housing benefit, arrears amounted to £9 million in March 1985 with over 45% of current tenants in arrears by an average of £265.
- Financial control systems are weak; and management lacks some of the basic information needed to manage its housing stock effectively.
- The deficit on the HRA amounted to over £15 million for 1984–85; this was in part due to the heavy staffing levels: the total cost of housing supervision and management in the authority exceeds £13 million a year; this is over £6 million a year more than might be expected in a metropolitan district with similar housing stock and socio-economic conditions after the effects of London Weighting are taken into account.

106. Of course, this is not a typical situation. Indeed, this report has cited evidence to suggest that local authorities' housing management performance compares quite favourably in some respects with that of housing associations and the private sector. Neither is it an isolated case; and it illustrates the problems that arise from lack of effective financial control. This chapter therefore deals in turn with the steps that the Commission considers need to be taken in housing authorities to:

(i) Set rents on the basis of the relevant facts.

(ii) Improve rent collection methods.

(iii) Keep arrears as low as possible, and recover amounts that may be due, at reasonable cost.

(iv) Control the costs of housing benefit administration.

(v) Provide members and officers with the information needed to manage the local housing stock effectively.

FIXING RENT LEVELS

107.   Rent levels are determined locally; and auditors and the Commission may not challenge policy decisions by authorities. However the Commission *does* have a legitimate concern to ensure that policy decisions are made on the basis of the relevant facts. Exhibit 13 shows that weekly rent for a 3-bedroom dwelling varies by a factor of over two to one. In one Outer London borough the weekly net rent (unrebated) is £13 and in another £24.50. The range is greater in Inner London and among shire districts; but even in metropolitan districts, the range is from £10.50 to £17.60 a week for a 3-bedroom dwelling.

Exhibit 13

UNREBATED RENT FOR A 3-BEDROOM COUNCIL HOUSE, APRIL 1985
£/week, in different housing authorities

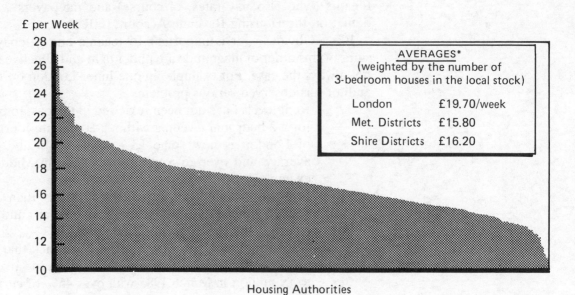

£ per Week

AVERAGES*	
(weighted by the number of 3-bedroom houses in the local stock)	
London	£19.70/week
Met. Districts	£15.80
Shire Districts	£16.20

Housing Authorities

* Excluding Kensington and Chelsea (65 homes, £44.90 a week)

Source: Audit Commission analysis of CIPFA Housing Rents Statistics,1985 Actuals

108.   The effect of decisions on local rent levels is far reaching:
   – They influence the level of service that can be afforded by the authority, in terms of maintenance and services for the elderly for example.
   – They affect local rate bills: for instance an average rent increase of £2 a week in the authority described in paragraph 105 would allow a reduction in local domestic rate bills of 16%, or 19p in the £.
   – They establish the opportunity cost for tenants considering the purchase of their dwellings, as is discussed later in this report. The breakeven rent for a 3-bedroom council dwelling valued at £22,000 and discounted by 50% is £25 a week at current (net) interest rates and including an allowance of £330 a year for external maintenance (and assuming that the purchaser is paying income tax at the standard rate). If the rent is lower than this, ignoring any possible capital appreciation, it will be cheaper to continue to rent rather than to buy. Since over 100 authorities charged less than £15 a week for a 3-bedroom dwelling in April 1985 (and only 40 charged £20 a week or more) it is perhaps not surprising that despite the very attractive discounts, around

two-thirds of council tenants not in receipt of housing benefit have yet to purchase their current dwelling. [Of course, other factors also influence tenants' decisions including their age and employment prospects and the type and condition of the property.]*

109.   The Commission recognises that these economic factors are often outweighed by political considerations: the effect on the disadvantaged of increased housing costs and the effect on voters. It is for local housing authorities to assess the appropriate balance, bearing in mind that at present in a typical metropolitan district 40% of tenants receive a certificated rent rebate and a further 30% are on standard rebate. So, modest rent increases do not necessarily amount to 'soaking the poor'; paradoxically, they are more likely to attract increased central support via the Exchequer for local housing improvements.

110.   The Commission has discussed the economic issues involved in setting rent levels in its report published in April 1985, *Capital Expenditure Controls in Local Government in England.* It recognises, too, that housing finance is a complex and contentious field in which it is unwise to consider one part of the housing market (council tenants) in isolation from the rest. This section draws attention to the economic consequences – in terms of the funds available for investment – of current rental policies in local authorities.

111.   Many local authorities have fixed rents at levels that are insufficient to keep buildings in good repair, as the maintenance backlog shows. Indeed, the Commission's earlier report on the block grant system examined Housing Revenue Accounts in 1983–84: 139 were in balance – but only in the sense that they were meeting the outgoings and debt charges on historic costs; 159 were in deficit, several by £300 or more per dwelling. Table 16 shows the Housing Revenue Account position last year for all council-owned dwellings in London, metropolitan and shire districts.

Table 16: RENTS AND HOUSING COSTS, 1984–5
£/week, average for all dwellings

	London £/week	Met. Districts £/week	Shire Districts £/week
Gross rent	17.1	13.7	14.9
Interest charges (gross)*	21.1	10.5	10.7
Management	6.9	2.7	3.0
Repairs/maintenance	7.2	4.5	5.3
Total costs	35.2	17.7	19.0
SURPLUS/(DEFICIT) per dwelling	(18.1)	(4.0)	(4.1)
[Memo: annual deficit per dwelling	£941	£208	£213]

* Before subsidy, interest receivable and non-rent income.

Even after subsidies, interest on capital receipts and non-rent income are credited, the average annual deficit per dwelling in London was almost £7 a week and that outside London approached £1.50.

112.   Of course, the situation differs between authorities, as Exhibit 13 showed. Nonetheless, the fact remains that on average rents are not covering outgoings; in London, they are not even covering historic capital costs. Moreover, in many cases rents are subsidised by interest on the proceeds from authorities' sales of land and buildings – introducing further distortions to the 'signals' given to the local housing market and to tenants.

* The metropolitan district with the highest average rent has sold over 20% of its stock to former tenants, even though it is among the 15 most deprived authorities outside London in housing terms.

113. As Hepworth *et al** observe, the Housing Revenue Account figures are relatively meaningless, since they ignore the replacement cost of the building. An authority which happens to have a relatively old stock of council property can balance its HRA account with relatively low rents, because it has low capital costs; an authority with relatively new housing stock will have to charge higher rents. As stated earlier, this approach means that authorities are not, in general, building up the funds needed to meet the costs of major refurbishments to properties. As a result, when major renovations are required (as is the case with many system-built houses now) the local authority and government face an unenviable choice between letting the fabric continue to deteriorate or placing an increased burden on the ratepayers. Often they choose the first option; so the maintenance backlog is the not-so-hidden cost of uneconomic rents.

114. In the discussion document referred to above, the concept of an economic rent for council housing is explored. This may be defined as the sum of depreciation on the property and the opportunity costs – the real annual return that the owner could expect if the dwelling is sold at its current capital value. On this basis, in 1980, the annual net economic rent for a typical local authority dwelling was just under £870 a year, using a 4% discount rate (as a proxy for the opportunity cost). In 1984 terms, the economic rent would be some £1,300, or £25 a week, for a typical local authority dwelling. In fact, as shown above, the average gross council house rent (i.e. before any rebates) outside London in 1984 was under £15 a week, of which supervision and management accounted for some £2.85.

115. In short, many local authorities are now charging rents around half the level necessary to cover the full economic cost of the dwelling. The consequences are clear: houses are not being properly maintained – which may well be one reason why opinion surveys show that many council tenants would prefer to be owner-occupiers; at the same time, the uneconomic rent reduces the incentive for tenants to buy their homes (in line with government policy) and inevitably restricts the supply of private rented accommodation. If local authorities felt able to charge rents closer to the levels necessary to cover the annual economic cost of the dwelling and could channel the extra income into capital repairs, the state of the local housing stock would be much improved.

116. Specifically, authorities (and so-called fair rents established by rent officers) should take account of the true economic cost and the need to maintain properties adequately when considering their rental policy. Too often, only the historic cost and its consequent effect on debt charges in the HRA is taken into account. This is one reason, no doubt, why the rents proposed in some refurbished houses on the Cantrel Farm estate at Knowsley (now Stockbridge Village) were recently *reduced* by some 20% by the local rent officer.

117. Relative rents also need to be examined. Often, they run counter to customer preferences. Rents are often related to original construction costs rather than their 'value' to tenants; so flats can be more expensive than houses of similar size, for example. This introduces distortions into the local market. One reason why void levels are high may be that rent on some difficult-to-let properties or estates is excessive relative to other council dwellings. Why should a tenant accept less desirable accommodation if a more desirable dwelling could become available soon at no extra cost? These anomalies can be corrected:
- Authorities such as Woking have long adjusted rent upwards on their more desirable estates.

* *Housing Rents, Costs and Subsidies*, Grey, Hepworth and Odling–Smee, March 1981.

- In Doncaster, an attempt is being made to put a 'value' on each property which can be taken into account when future rent levels are determined; alternatively the gross rateable value as assessed by the local District Valuer can be used.
- In North Devon, the council was so dissatisfied with maintenance performance that it decided to increase rents sharply, as shown in Exhibit 14. The additional income was channelled into a six year planned maintenance cycle costing on average £1,400 per dwelling and a £75 tenants' improvement grant. The result is better maintained properties, more economic maintenance arrangements (response maintenance is targeted to account for around 20% of the total maintenance workload, compared with over 50% a few years ago) and – the extra rent notwithstanding – tenants appear generally more satisfied.

Exhibit 14

NORTH DEVON DISTRICT COUNCIL RENTS, 1975-1985
Average rents for dwelling, at April 1
Index: April 1975 = 100

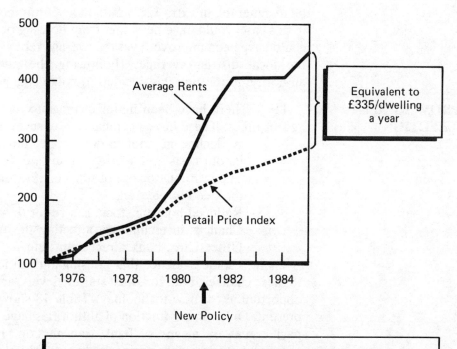

Between April 1978 and April 1985, rent in North Devon rose 15% faster than in the rest of Devon.
In the same period HRA maintenance and repairs expenditure increased nearly twice as fast.

Source: North Devon District Council Digest of Statistics
and CIPFA HRA Statistics

118. The situation in one larger-than-average shire district with a total insured dwelling value of £300 million is instructive. Average gross rental income per dwelling in 1984–85 was almost 50% lower than the average for the other neighbouring shire districts in the county. The council was spending around £1 million a year less than it needed to on the maintenance of its stock; and it reported in 1985 that it needed to spend up to £11 million

on the renewal of external doors and windows alone. Table 17 below shows that average weekly rent was not related to the gross rateable value (RV) of the property as assessed by the district valuer; the final column shows the weekly rent that would result from the application to the assessed value of a standard multiplier currently applied to the lowest value dwellings (4.9 times the valuation). Using the same multiplier throughout would ensure that the tenants of all the councils' dwellings are treated equally in terms of relative rent levels.

Table 17: RENT LEVELS RELATED TO RATEABLE VALUE, 1984–5
Illustrative example

Properties' Assessed Rateable Value (RV) £	Actual Rent/week £	Annual Rent as multiple of RV	Weekly Rent as 4.9 × Rateable Value £
87–121	10.41	4.9	10.41
122–152	10.81	3.8	13.80
153–182	11.25	3.2	16.80
183–212	11.79	2.9	19.80
213–242	12.54	2.6	22.80
243–272	13.22	2.5	25.80

[Calculation assumes a 48-week rent year]
Source: District Auditor's Report to the Local Authority.

The effect of the move to basing rents on assessed rateable values would be to generate an extra £2.75 million a year in income, of which some 45% in this case would have been met from housing benefit. Maintenance levels could have been improved; yet the average rent would still have been below the local district average. [Following the auditor's report, the local authority in question has decided to make changes along these lines.]

IMPROVING RENT COLLECTION

119.   There have been major changes to methods of rent collection in recent times. These have been caused by several factors:-
- A decline in door-to-door collection in response to increasing labour costs and a rising crime rate.
- The introduction of housing benefit, removing from many tenants the need to pay rent.
- Reduced housing stock as a result of sales.
- Changes in technology affecting the transmission of cash (Post Office Giro, bank direct debit, etc.).

There is some evidence that housing authorities have been slow to react to these changes, both to adjust staffing levels, and to take advantage of the opportunities of new technology. Table 18 shows how rent is collected at present. Only a small fraction of authorities have more than 10% of tenants paying rent by means of bank transmission. Post Office Giro is more common but again only a minority of authorities make significant use of this method.

Table 18: METHODS OF RENT PAYMENT, 1983–4
% tenants using different methods

	Shire Districts	Met. Districts	Outer London Boroughs	Inner London Boroughs
Cash office	29%	31	22	40
Door to door	28	24	2	—*
Post Office Giro	13	13	42	30
Bankers order	4	1	6	4
Other methods	1	2	2	3
Full housing benefit cases	25	29	26	23
TOTAL	100	100	100	100

* Very small

120.   The Commission's auditors are carrying out local projects examining local authority cash flow management. The results will be published later in the year. The present study compared different rent collection methods. Although the results are based on a limited sample of authorities, it is still possible to draw some general conclusions:

- Where tenants have bank accounts this is an inexpensive method of payment and reduces the probability of tenants cancelling a payment, particularly where variable direct debit is used.
- A higher level of door-to-door rent collection is associated with a lower level of arrears. 100% door-to-door collection would appear to reduce arrears expressed as a proportion of gross debit by a percentage point. However, the cost effectiveness of fortnightly door-to-door collectors depends on the number of calls per day and on the payment recording system. They can be effective in containing arrears and in maintaining observance of tenancy conditions if the collectors can be motivated to do this.
- Collection by caretakers and wardens is inexpensive; and rent collection reinforces their estate management role. But the risk of assault and theft needs to be considered; it is higher in urban areas.
- Fortnightly collection via a Giro-designated Post Office system is particularly cost-effective. However, weekly collection doubles the cost and may not be cost-effective. In any case, where the Post Office is *not* designated and data is sent to authorities via the Giro centres at Bootle there can be significant delays. Authorities may need to monitor Giro charges and review the choice of method if there are significant increases.
- Some rural authorities negotiate favourable terms for collection of rent at local parish council offices.

121.   Nearly all authorities carry out rent accounting with some degree of computer assistance. Only 14% of authorities (almost entirely Shire districts) are still using a manual system. The type of system varies widely, however, as does the range of facilities provided. In part, this is because rent accounting was often the first activity computerised in many housing departments; and many systems are now relatively antiquated even though sometimes less than ten years old. For example, older systems might not provide for on-line interrogation of tenants' files from local cash offices and typically might only update accounts weekly or fortnightly – nearly 20% of systems do not provide on-line access, and 10% update tenant accounts less frequently than weekly. As a result, the type and range of management information possible may be limited. Some ways to ensure that management information systems are adequate will be discussed later, in paragraphs 134–137.

ARREARS PREVENTION AND RECOVERY

122.   There is little point in determining appropriate rent levels for individual dwellings if the sums involved cannot be collected. At present there is a disturbingly wide variation in the level of arrears. Even when account is taken of factors outside the control of authorities, such as local, social and economic characteristics, the level of arrears can vary at the extreme by a factor of 30 when the best and worst are compared.

123.   The Commission's previous report on arrears: *Bringing Council Tenants' Arrears Under Control* (HMSO, March 1984), examined the position in London, the metropolitan districts and the 28 largest shire districts in terms of population. It recorded a sharp deterioration in the position in the three years to September 1983 with a few authorities having particular problems. (The 12 Inner London boroughs and ten housing

authorities outside London, accounted for almost half of total arrears of the 95 authorities studied). The report stressed that the priority for management should be to prevent arrears accumulating; prevention being far more effective than recovery. It also set out a series of practical steps that authorities could be taking to contain the problem.

124.   The current study has reviewed the position in the authorities covered in the previous study, to determine what improvements have been made; it has also examined the remaining shire districts. In *all* authorities, total current and former tenants' arrears at March 1984 stood at nearly £250 million. Although the overall magnitude of the problem is not as great in the smaller authorities as in the metropolitan districts and London authorities included in the earlier study, there is nonetheless in aggregate outstanding unpaid rent of over £65 million in these authorities. Total rent arrears at the end of March 1985 amounted to the equivalent of some 25 days rent on average, but in 262 authorities arrears amount to under 3% of gross debit (less than 10 days rent), and 168 authorities have arrears under 2%. Many housing associations have arrears in the range 2–3% of gross debit and nearly all manage a smaller number of dwellings. For those authorities covered by the previous study, Exhibit 15 shows, by type of

Exhibit 15

TRENDS IN TENANTS' ARREARS, 1981-1984

**Arrears as % of gross debit in different classes of authority
(82 of the largest authorities, representing 50% of the total stock)**

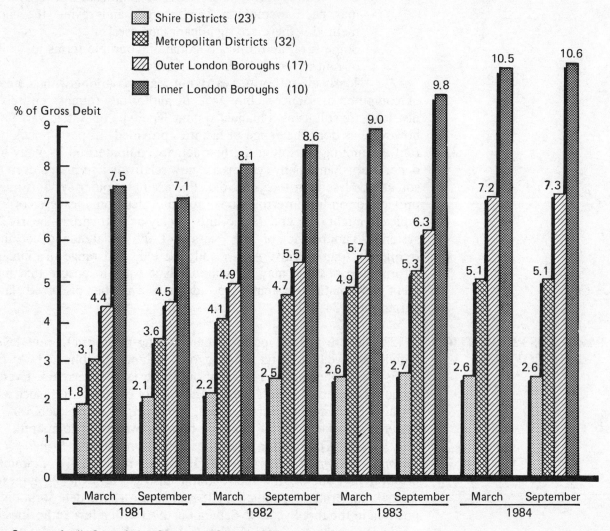

Source: Audit Commission Surveys, 1984 and 1985

authority, the change in the average level of arrears expressed as a percentage of the gross debit from March 1981 to September 1984. Although the interpretation is complicated by the introduction of the housing benefit scheme in November 1982 and April 1983, some immediate observations can be made.

- The rising trend in the metropolitan and the large shire districts has been halted since the Commission's first report. Between March 1981 and September 1983 arrears had been rising steadily. Since September 1983 the trend in these authorities has been, if anything, downwards.

- This is confirmed by analysis of the changes between September 1983 and September 1984 in the 95 largest housing authorities in England and Wales. As Table 19 shows, outside London in six out of every seven authorities surveyed, arrears as a proportion of gross debit had either reduced or remained steady.

Table 19: CHANGE IN TENANTS' ARREARS: SEPTEMBER 1984 VS SEPTEMBER 1983
Based on % gross annual debit – largest authorities

	Shire Districts	Met. Districts	Outer London Boroughs	Inner London Boroughs
Reduction	13	18	8	4
No (or <0.5%) change	12	12	6	2
Increase				
0.5 to 1.5%	3	4	2	1
1.5 to 2.5%	—	—	—	4
2.5 to 3.5%	—	—	2	—
over 3.5%	—	1	2	1
Total authorities	28	35	20	12
[Memo: % of these authorities with increased arrears	11	14	30	50]

- Excluding the worst 11 authorities, the favourable trend has been maintained since September 1984. Reported arrears in all classes of authority were lower in March 1985 than they had been a year earlier. Arrears in September 1985 in 17 of a sample* of 24 large housing authorities were lower than they had been in September 1984, and in a further 4 the situation was substantially unchanged; only in 3 of the 24* authorities had the situation worsened.

- But in the worst 11 authorities in terms of rent arrears, a bad situation is continuing to worsen, as Table 20 demonstrates.

Table 20: ELEVEN AUTHORITIES WITH HIGH ARREARS
Total arrears as % Gross Debit to end September

	Average		
	1983	1984	1985
Worst Eleven Authorities	13.0%	15.4	17.5
Other Large Authorities	6.3	6.5	6.1

- There is evidence that some authorities in Inner London are not devoting sufficient effort to arrears control. The average number of staff on arrears control per 1,000 cases in Inner London is only two-thirds of the overall average.

- The trends discussed above are even more disturbing since they relate arrears to gross debit. In fact, the proportion of rent collectable is falling as more tenants have either all or part of the

---

* The authorities were selected on the basis of either total arrears over £2 million or greater than 5% of gross debit, at September 1984.

rent paid by housing benefit. (In many authorities, approaching 70% of all tenants receive at least some housing benefit). For instance, reported arrears in Brent at the end of March 1985 were £5.3 million, or 33.5% of annual gross debit; but this represented some 60% or *more* of the rent due annually directly from tenants.

125.   The 'true' arrears position is thus masked, to some extent, by the effect of housing benefit. The distortion is not all one way, however. The actual level of arrears, as measured by rent unpaid, may be an over-statement if many tenants would be on housing benefit but for inefficiencies in the systems for assessing eligibility for benefit. In a number of authorities there are significant delays in benefit assessment. Housing officers have often been unable to deal effectively with arrears cases because they have been unable to distinguish between those who are genuinely in arrears and those whose arrears will be eliminated or reduced by housing benefit payments. In one authority, examination of a sample of cases shown as being in arrears indicated that only 38% were 'true' arrears cases; 46% were awaiting housing benefit assessment by the local DHSS (Social Security office) and 16% were waiting for clearance for direct bank credit. Delays in benefit assessments therefore effect the level of arrears. However, the benefit system itself has not even been as effective in reducing arrears as it might have been. Authorities need still to collect small amounts from many tenants on benefit (e.g. for the residual rents of standard recipients and items such as garage rents). Although 66% of tenants receive some housing benefit assistance, only 26% make no additional rent payment at present. Collection of these small amounts can be almost as time-consuming as collecting the original full rent.

126.   The recommendations of the Commission's earlier (March 1984) report are even more relevant now. It is important that:

(i)   Members should give clear policy guidelines for arrears control and recovery (but, not involve themselves in details of individual cases).

(ii)   With the possible exception only of the smallest authorities, responsibility for rent collection and accounting should be concentrated in the housing department and not separated from it, in another department.

(iii)   Accurate and timely information must be available to officers responsible for managing arrears. Rent payment methods and computerised rent accounting systems must enable non-payment to be recognised before the next rent is due.

(iv)   Tenants must know where they stand. It is difficult to blame tenants for non-payment (especially with the confusion caused by housing benefit in many areas) if they do not know how much they owe.

(v)   Authorities must take action promptly to prevent arrears escalating to the point where recovery is unlikely.

(vi)   The actions must be fair but firm. Distraint of goods or the serving of 'notice seeking possession' must be followed through where necessary with the full support of members.

(vii)   Full advantage should be taken of the housing benefit arrangements where tenants are unable to afford rent.

(viii)   Specialist arrears recovery staff should be employed where appropriate: generic housing officers can often have conflicting priorities and assigned staff should be adequately trained in debt counselling in order to provide tenants with advice where necessary.

(ix)   As discussed in Chapter One, housing management in large urban areas should be decentralised with local staff responsible for all aspects of housing; particular estates should be assigned to individual officers with defined performance targets.

In light of these recommendations and of auditor's efforts to persuade authorities to take action over the past 18 months it is particularly disturbing that the situation in London has continued to deteriorate generally over the past two years as Exhibit 16 shows – despite the impressive performance of some authorities in the capital.

127.   The choice of method used to control arrears is clearly a matter of local choice. But some authorities are much more successful than others in containing the problem by applying the above procedures with appropriate firmness:

– Sedgefield, for example, has a policy to start proceedings for distraint of goods in lieu of rent using bailiffs as soon as arrears are outstanding more than 2 or 3 weeks. With the full support of members, and appropriate safeguards for those unable to pay, actual current arrears have reduced over the last 18 months since the policy was introduced by nearly 50% (although at least part of this reduction is attributable to housing benefit).

Exhibit 16

TRENDS IN ARREARS IN LONDON

Arrears as % of gross debit

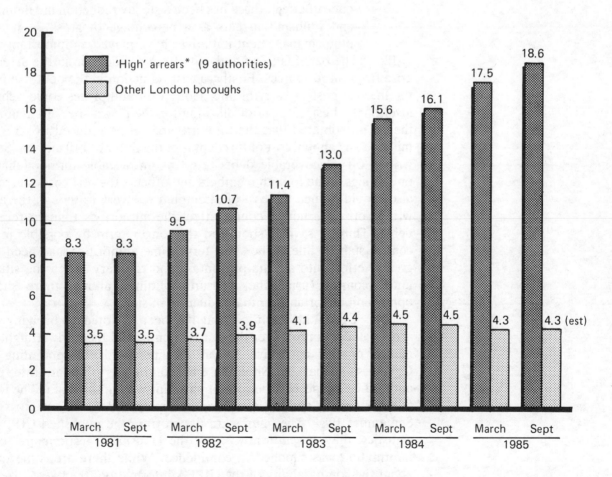

* Authorities with total arrears > 10% of gross debit at September 1984

Source: Audit Commission Surveys, 1984 and 1985 and auditors' returns, 1986

- Wigan issues a notice seeking possession (NSP) when arrears are outstanding for more than 4 weeks following intermediate warnings. The effectiveness is shown by the results: in 1984–85 4,500 NSP's were issued but nearly 90% of these tenants subsequently complied with agreements to reduce the arrears by mutually acceptable amounts. Of those cases finally presented to court only approximately 50 tenants were eventually evicted for non-payment. Wigan has substantially lower arrears than most other metropolitan districts.
- Hammersmith and Fulham have adopted an incentive approach on an experimental basis. All tenants, whose arrears in a 13 week monitoring period to May 1985 were more than 8 weeks net charges, were to receive a further increase in rent from July 1 1985 over and above the normal increase that applied from April 1 unless:

  - *either* rent arrears were reduced below 8 weeks net charges or to under £200.

  - *or* the arrears were reduced during the 13 weeks by 25%.

  - *or* the tenant entered into an agreement for the beginning of the 13 week period to pay their current rent plus an agreed sum of the arrears, and adhered to the terms of the agreement for the whole of the 13 week period.

  Some 850 out of 1,340 (i.e. 63%) tenants seriously in arrears took one of these steps as a result of the threat of a maximum rent increase of £3 a week. This does not appear to have been a one-off effect: there has been a steady reduction in Hammersmith and Fulham's arrears as a percentage of gross debit although other management initiatives have played an important role.

128. The benefits to an authority from a reduction in the arrears level arise from three sources. Firstly, a cost reduction in the debt itself reduces the interest cost of carrying the debt. If all authorities could achieve the level of the best 25%, after allowing for their own special circumstances, then it is estimated that the total arrears can be reduced by 35%, or £85 million. The annual cost of this debt is of the order of £10 million. Secondly, writing off irrecoverable debts (e.g. for untraceable former tenants) not only brings home to both members and officers the real cost of arrears, but also should reduce the cost of attempted recovery (although the action of writing-off does not of course affect the authority's right to recover the debt). Thirdly, savings should in the longer term be possible in arrears control staff. While in the short term some authorities may need to put a greater effort into arrears prevention and recovery, when the situation is under control (using the measures outlined above) there should be opportunities for an eventual reduction in staff.

129. Given the attention that has been devoted to bringing tenants' arrears under control over the last 18 months and the fairly straightforward nature of the corrective action required it is disappointing to the Commission that the situation has continued to deteriorate in some authorities – especially because it has improved in the main. The following table lists those authorities where arrears exceeded 10% of gross debit in September 1984. The figures are drawn from the published CIPFA HRA statistics; they are *not* drawn from the Housing Questionnaire for which information was supplied in confidence. While there are some questions about the comparability of the CIPFA information, the overall trends and level of arrears are indicative.

Table 21: ELEVEN AUTHORITIES WITH HIGHEST ARREARS
Total arrears as % of rent roll at end of March

	1983	1984	1985
Brent	23.2	31.4	33.5
Lambeth	21.1*	20.8	24.0
Haringey	18.5	13.2	15.2
Islington	17.4	14.5	15.1
Southwark	13.5	17.2	20.5
Lewisham	12.9	20.3	22.3
Walsall	12.1	13.9	14.4
Hackney	10.2	10.9	27.2
Liverpool	9.7	11.8	12.0
Camden	9.6	9.9	11.2
Waltham Forest	8.1	16.5	17.8
Average	14.2	16.4	19.4

* Estimates
Source: Returns to DOE

Most of the authorities cited above are in Inner London, and most saw an increase in arrears between March 1983 and March 1985. Together, these authorities' arrears in March 1985 totalled over £100 million, 40% of the national total. It is in these authorities that effort needs to be concentrated in the near-term.

CONTROLLING HOUSING BENEFIT ADMINISTRATION

130.   The Housing Benefits Scheme first introduced in November 1982, whereby the responsibility for most aspects of housing benefit administration was transferred to the local authorities, was intended to make net savings in manpower of up to 400 posts nationally. As the report* of the House of Commons Committee of Public Accounts makes clear, these savings have not been realised. The Explanatory and Financial Memorandum to the *Social Security and Housing Benefits Bill* estimated that authorities would require 1,500 to 1,600 extra staff to implement the system. Authorities' own estimates for 1983–84 suggested that the true figure would be over 2,500 extra staff. In fact, the latest estimated figure is now 3,500. This more than offsets the reduction achieved in Civil Service manpower in 1983–84 of some 2,400 (itself offset by about 500 extra posts needed to deal with increased take-up of supplementary benefit consequent on the introduction of housing benefit). The Public Accounts Committee recognised the difficulties faced by authorities in dealing with unexpectedly complex cases and with the increase in take-up, but they expressed concern that the requirements for extra staff are more than double the original estimate.

131.   Analysis of the effect of housing benefit and the cost of administering the system is difficult. The figures for tenants receiving rent and rate rebates need to be separated from private tenants receiving rate rebates and rent allowances and from benefit payments to owner-occupiers. Even the number of tenants in receipt of rebates varies during the year as the qualifying conditions and personal circumstances of tenants change. (The situation seems likely to change again, as a result of the government proposals set out in the recent White Paper.) With these provisos, Table 22 shows that there is relatively little difference between classes of authority in the proportion of tenants receiving all or part of their rent payment as housing benefit.

These figures must be interpreted with care, however. In some authorities the proportion of tenants in receipt of housing benefit may be lower than in others because relatively low rent levels have been set.

---

* 6th report from the Committee of Public Accounts – Session 1984–5: Housing Benefit Scheme, HMSO 1985.

Table 22: PROPORTION OF LOCAL AUTHORITY TENANTS IN RECEIPT OF RENT REBATES, %

	Shire Districts	Met. Districts	Outer London Boroughs	Inner London Boroughs
Certificated rebates	34%	40	33	33
Standard rebates	33	31	31	24
	67	71	64	57

132.   It is even more difficult to establish the true cost of administration of the council rent rebate element of housing benefit. Often the same staff, usually in the finance department, deal with all aspects including rate rebates and rent allowances. Thus, estimates have had to be made of the proportion of staff time and costs attributable solely to council tenant rent rebates. It could be misleading to select one part of the system for examination in isolation; but the following observations are relevant:

- The average annual administrative cost per local authority recipient overall was £11.60 in 1983–84. But in the lowest 25% of authorities the cost was only £6.60. If all authorities were to reach this cost level the annual cost saving would be £15 million approximately.

- These calculations relate to the average number of recipients in the year. In fact the number of cases dealt with will be higher because of the need to recalculate entitlement as family circumstances change e.g. losing or gaining a job, and revisions brought about by changes to rent levels and pensions. However these qualifications apply to all authorities, including the lowest-cost 25%.

- Although these costs are currently met by the DHSS, the longer term proposals are to include a standard allowance for housing benefit administration in the rate support grant settlement. Increases in local efficiency would therefore be in the authorities' own interests. Staffing levels (and costs) should of course be adequate to ensure that cases are dealt with in accordance with the timescale required by the housing benefit regulations.

133.   Further work is being carried out by a joint Audit Commission/ CIPFA working party in establishing the current position, workload and problems in the administration of housing benefit. Present indications from this work are that there are severe continuing problems at a good number of authorities. There is an evident need for a statement of good practice in housing benefit administration which the joint working party are to produce and which will be published shortly. In any event, the housing authorities where annual housing benefit administration costs per recipient currently exceed £10 should initiate detailed investigation to see why they cannot match the performance of the better authorities.

BETTER MANAGEMENT INFORMATION

134.   Without sound management information, tight financial and operating control will not be possible. Three steps would help to ensure that members and officers have the information that they need for housing management purposes:

(i) General application of the findings of the Institute of Housing Working Party on Computerisation of Housing Functions.

(ii) Universal adoption of the CIPFA guidelines on the treatment of central establishment charges in Housing Revenue Accounts.

(iii) An urgent review of the conventions governing capital accounting in local government *before* any regulations are issued on the form of local authorities' statutory accounts.

Each of these steps is discussed briefly below.

Computerisation of housing management information

135. The management of housing requires accurate and timely information on a house-by-house and tenant-by-tenant basis, on such things as rent payments, occupancy, housing benefit, and maintenance requested and carried out. This information needs to be available to estate management staff weekly. In most authorities, such information can only be provided using computers. And decentralisation, to whatever degree, requires effective computing facilities, to give management both at the 'centre' and in the areas the information that is needed. 'On line' access by area staff to the rent accounts, waiting and transfer lists, and allocations need to be considered when decentralisation is in prospect: a reasonable maxim would be 'no decentralisation without computerisation'.

136. The present level of computerisation is mixed. Only 18% of authorities have fully computerised the four key housing functions of rent accounting, waiting list administration and lettings, maintenance, and housing benefit. A further 70% have two or three of these computerised and 12% only one or none. Many authorities are actively planning either to introduce or to upgrade such systems, and the opportunity should be taken to design in a greater level of integration.

137. An Institute of Housing working party, sponsored by a consortium of local authorities and housing associations, has examined the computerisation of housing functions. It has recently produced an outline specification for housing systems which authorities considering changing their computer hardware and software should study; it is based on the experience of authorities with successful computer applications. The specification is particularly useful in providing a framework against which authorities can decide how best to introduce computers, building up eventually to a fully integrated computer system for most if not all housing functions if required. The general principles associated with successful implementation of a computer system are well known. In summary, it is essential that housing authorities:

(a) Are fully committed to the success of the system at all levels of staff.

(b) Carry out a rigorous cost-benefit appraisal in order to establish the appropriate options for the individual authority.

(c) Consider the relative merits of purpose-built developments and (the adaptation of) commercial packages.

(d) Recognise that the computer system must be capable of accommodating changes as circumstances change and experience increases.

(e) Co-operate fully with the development staff so that the system meets their requirements – the client must be in charge.

(f) Plan for, and control, the changeover to the new system and allow sufficient time for training.

(g) Ensure that staff are familiar with computing, perhaps by experiments with micro computers.

(h) And finally, are aware that computing systems nearly always bring pain and trouble before reward!

At minimum, the Chairman of any Committee authorising expenditure on computer hardware or software in the housing context should be satisfied that the lessons set out in the IOH working party report *Computerisation of Housing Functions* are not going to be re-learned unnecessarily at tenants' and ratepayers' expense.

Adoption of CIPFA guidelines on accounting for central charges

138. In addition to making full use of computers, accounting standards for council housing income and expenditure need to be reviewed. Housing authorities should as a matter of course, be active in monitoring their own performance in relation to their peers. But this is particularly difficult because of the great variation in the way accounts are prepared and presented. During the course of the study, considerable effort was required by the study team, auditors and local authority staff to ensure that the data were strictly comparable so that valid conclusions could be drawn. There is a clear need for a national accounting and reporting standard for the Housing Revenue Account, to be adhered to by all housing authorities. Although CIPFA has published guidelines* for the accounting treatment of various items of expenditure, they have not always been followed strictly, in many cases.

139. Specifically, there is a need to define more clearly the information presented in the Housing Revenue Account. All central costs charged to the Housing Revenue Account should be separately identified. Indeed this approach to identification of services with recharges is one which the Commission considers essential across the whole span of local authorities' activities. The very title of Central Establishment Charges fosters the wrong attitude which is compounded by the customary process of apportionment of costs. At best there is a weakness in control and accountability for these charges. At worst, the arrangements are seen by service departments as the dumping on them of expenditure (to be met from often hard-pressed budgets) over which they have no control and which they cannot relate to services provided or value added. Yet there is a ready solution. The approach outlined in paragraph 28 will fit in well with the accounting structure already recommended by CIPFA. In the case of housing, the recharges for services of central departments – finance, legal and secretarial, architectural, engineering, typing etc. – appear as a standard group in the Supervision and Management Holding Account supporting the main Housing Revenue Account. These recommendations should be universal practice. The supporting information for these charges should be in sufficient detail to link the charges with the services provided (for example, servicing debt, paying bills, legal action on arrears etc.). That detailed information should also be provided to the chief housing officer for the purposes already explained.

Urgent review of capital accounting conventions

140. Except for direct labour organisations, depreciation is not a feature of local government accounting. Local authorities are governed by legal and accounting conventions which are different from those relating to limited companies. The starting point is that local authorities must meet all expenditure from revenue within the year unless there is power to carry it forward. They have no capital as such. Carrying forward needs a borrowing power or its equivalent. So, instead of buying an asset and providing through depreciation for its eventual replacement, the local authority convention is that the asset is provided out of loans to be repaid over a period approximating to the life of the asset. At the end of the life of the asset any replacement would need a new decision and new borrowing. This worked well when things were simple and the figures relatively small. Annual loan charges were an approximation of the rate of consumption of the asset. Residual values were always ignored – but that did not matter too much.

141. However many complications have now crept in. Through lack of maintenance, assets are being consumed at a faster rate than provision is

---

* E.g. *The 1985 Standard Classification Service Guidance Booklet – Housing and Other Services* (CIPFA, August 1985).

made for the payment for them. In the case of Ronan Point, for instance, the asset has been totally consumed in 20 years but loan repayments will go on for another 40. As a result the whole area of local authority capital financing and accounting now needs a thorough re-examination – on the lines of that carried out for the water industry prior to the creation of the water authorities. In that case, the Woodham Committee recommended changes to a depreciation basis and that proposal was adopted.

142.   The Commission urges that such a review should be undertaken urgently by the government in consultation with CIPFA and the Local Authority Associations. The review will need to cover the question of outstanding maintenance and refurbishment and how those liabilities are to be treated in the accounts – in most cases the backlog of maintenance and improvement (which now totals some £20 billion nationwide) greatly exceeds the provision made for meeting the cost of repairs. Clearly this is a particularly difficult issue but it is important that the facts are brought out into the open. For this reason, and pending the examination of the whole capital accounting issue, the Commission takes the view that backlogs of repair and refurbishment work needed on the housing stock – as well as profiles of further needs arising over a rolling ten year period – should be assessed by each housing authority and clearly set out in its *Annual Report*.

143.   The need for a comprehensive review of local government asset accounting is particularly timely. First, inadequate maintenance of local authority capital assets has resulted in a large backlog of repairs which is not reflected in the accounts – which thus give a misleading impression of the financial health of housing authorities. Second, unless users understand – and pay – the full cost of occupying land and buildings they will have less incentive to ensure that these are put to the best possible use in the public interest. Finally, government has proposed to issue regulations on the form of local authority statutory accounts; and it would be most unfortunate if these regulations fail to address the key accounting issues to be resolved.

* * *

So far, this report has urged a managerial solution to the crisis facing public housing in England and Wales. Table 23 suggests some indicators of the efficiency of local housing authorities, to complement these on economy [in Chapter 1] and effectiveness [in Chapter 2]. As with all general, first level, indicators included in this report every authority has received more detailed feedback on its relative performance via its auditors.

Table 23:   PROPOSED HOUSING MANAGEMENT PERFORMANCE INDICATORS: EFFICIENCY

	Benchmark	Cause for Concern
Annual rent as % market valuation	6%	4%
Arrears as % gross debit	2%	4%
Housing benefit administration cost per recipient	£7/year	£10
On-line information on		
– rent payments	Yes	No
– voids	Yes	No
– maintenance response times	Yes	No

The report has suggested that the situation can be improved, materially, with the resources that are now available. The Commission believes that in many authorities, better management can indeed make a substantial difference especially if combined with tighter financial control and a commitment to providing better services for tenants. But it would be naive to suggest that these measures will be adequate to meet all the problems inherited from the past. Exhibit 17 shows that even on optimistic assumptions about the value improvements that could be generated from implementation of the recommendations in this report, little immediate headway would be made in clearing the £20 billion repairs and improvements backlog. The most that could be reasonably expected after a 2–3 year implementation period would be of the order of £1 billion a year. Moreover, local management may not be able to cope with the challenges involved. In such circumstances proposing a managerial solution may be tantamount to suggesting a rearrangement of the deckchairs on the Titanic. More radical approaches may be required. Some possibilities that appear worthy of consideration by all concerned are therefore discussed in the final chapter of this report.

Exhibit 17

OPTIMISTIC PROJECTIONS,
AFTER 3 YEARS

**POTENTIAL VALUE IMPROVEMENTS FROM
BETTER HOUSING MANAGEMENT**
£m, at **1984** prices

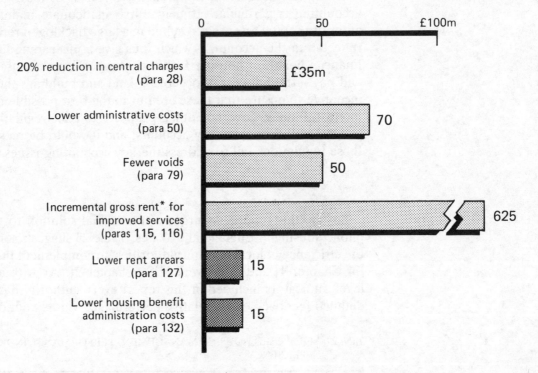

* Assumes an average increase of £2.50/week

72

4. Encouraging new approaches to funding and managing public housing

144.　The Commission is concerned that the steps so far proposed in this report may not produce the necessary improvements in the state of council housing, for three main reasons: the necessary funds may not be available; authorities may insist on adopting a 'go it alone' strategy, without the resources to carry it through; and/or authorities may simply not be up to the managerial challenges involved.

145.　However, it will be evident from the three preceding chapters that it is not appropriate to treat all housing authorities as though they were all facing the same problems or are equally competent (or incompetent) to manage them. As Exhibit 18 suggests, authorities can be segmented into three distinct categories:

(a)　Those facing relatively few housing problems (as shown by the authorities' housing Z-score) which are at least competently managed. About 260 authorities, mostly shire districts, accounting for over 50% of the total council-owned stock of dwellings fall into this category. The Commission believes that given appropriate freedom to manage, authorities in this Category (A) have adequate resources and should not need to borrow further to meet local housing needs.

Exhibit 18

CLASSIFICATION OF HOUSING AUTHORITIES, 1984
Number of authorities in each 'box', and % of total housing stock

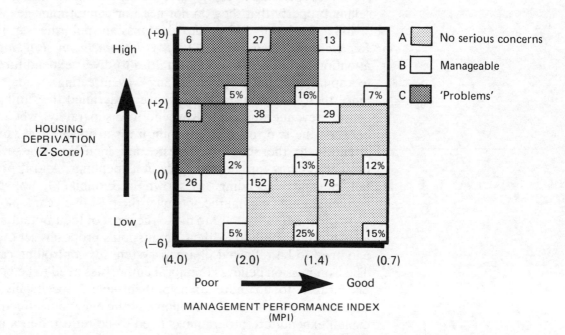

Source:　Management Performance based on Analysis as described in Appendix B
Housing Z-scores from Department of Environment

(b) Approximately 80 authorities which should be able to deal with local housing problems given access to future capital receipts, ability to borrow at the levels approved over the past 2–3 years and a willingness to tap private sources of funds (Category B).

(c) Problem authorities with a local shortage of rented accommodation, very serious problems with the current housing stock inherited from the mistakes of the past and limited potential for asset sales. Perhaps 40 authorities fall into this Category (C). If the daunting housing problems in these areas are to be tackled effectively, additional public expenditure is likely to be required at the very minimum to attract new private sector funding.

For a further 12 authorities there was insufficient information supplied on the questionnaire to form a view of their management performance.

146. This chapter covers the steps that the Commission considers need to be taken *over and above those described in the previous three chapters* to help the three classes of authority identified above to meet their funding requirements:

(i) Relax the current controls over local authorities' ability to fund capital spending internally, from the sale of assets. This should meet most of the external funding needs of Category A authorities.

(ii) Attract more private sector finance. This will be essential in Category B authorities where saleable assets and local property market values will not be sufficient to generate the necessary funds internally to meet the authorities' capital needs.

(iii) Invest more public resources in Category C problem authorities, if only to attract the necessary weight of private money to tackle the serious problems involved.

INTERNAL FUNDING OF HOUSING IMPROVEMENTS

147. Given the scale of their present housing problems, authorities must be able to make full use of their existing resources. At present, the way in which central government seeks to control (separately) individual authorities' revenue and capital spending has had the perverse effect of simultaneously preventing major shifts in resources from day-to-day (revenue) spending to capital investment and discouraging authorities from selling property that they do not need or cannot manage.

148. In April 1985, the Commission published a report, *Capital Expenditure Controls in Local Government in England* which drew attention to the sizeable opportunities to divert expenditure from revenue to capital spending without in any way affecting standards and service. Since then, events in Liverpool have underlined the futility of seeking to control revenue and capital expenditure separately, when the distinction between the two forms of expenditure is artificial. The same report drew attention to the substantial waste and inefficiency associated with the present systems for controlling capital spending. And it projected a large fall in capital spending, as shown in Exhibit 19, notwithstanding the accumulation of capital receipts over the past five years, of over £6 billion.

149. If authorities are to make the most of their potential for improving local housing conditions, the Commission's proposals set out almost a year ago need to be reflected in a new system for controlling capital spending. The Commission believes that local authorities need to be both enabled and encouraged to do more to help themselves. Specifically, the following requirements basic to the economy, efficiency and effectiveness of local capital expenditure programmes need to be reflected in a new approach:

(i) A 3–5 year planning horizon for capital, so that programmes and projects are not subject to abrupt changes and the year-end 'rush to spend'.

(ii) Adequate provision for replenishment of fixed assets in accounting treatment and spending programmes.

(iii) Encouragement to authorities to do more for themselves to fund their capital programmes and to rely less on new borrowing as a source of capital finance.

(iv) Minimal central involvement in the details of local programmes and projects. Unless projects are large (i.e. costing over £5 million, say) and/or cannot be funded internally, there seems little case for mandatory project controls.

(v) Continued incentives to authorities to dispose of under-utilised assets – even though special arrangements may be needed to deal with the problem of the 'over-hanging' £6 billion of past capital receipts.

(vi) Simplification of the system, in particular to avoid the need to distinguish between revenue and capital expenditure for control purposes. Revenue and capital are obviously inter-related and authorities face a choice between them (i.e. higher capital costs now, lower revenue costs later; less capital investment now, higher revenue expenditure later). This calls into question any system that seeks to control the two forms of expenditure separately. The present arrangements are a recipe for unproductive 'creative accounting'.

Exhibit 19   *ILLUSTRATIVE*

**PROJECTED CAPITAL PROGRAMME UNDER
EXISTING CONTROL SYSTEM**

Best Estimates — £ billions

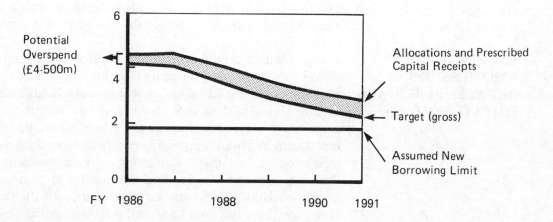

Source: Audit Commission report:
Capital Expenditure Controls in Local Government in England, 1985

150. The Commission is pleased to note that some, at least, of these requirements are reflected in the Government's recent Green Paper, *Paying for Local Government*. But some of these basic requirements will not be met if the Green Paper's proposals are enacted as they stand; and the Commission will be commenting in detail in due course.

151. In particular, as the Commission's report referred to above made clear, there remains considerable potential for further asset sales. While many authorities, some with severe local housing problems, have sold up to 25% of their stock to tenants, the average is under 15%. However, at

present authorities are not able to use more than 20% of their capital receipts from the sale of council houses or 30% of their receipts from the sale of non-housing assets in any single year to finance capital improvements to housing; and every authority's aggregate capital spending is subject to detailed central control. As a result, it is likely that over the medium term the trend in asset sales will be downwards unless changes are made. Table 24 below shows the Commission's best estimate last April of receipts over the next six years from housing sales, mortgage sales and other sources.

Table 24: BEST ESTIMATE OF CAPITAL RECEIPTS
England, £ billion

	Housing Sales	Mortgage Sales	Other	Total
FY 1986	£1.4bn	0.2	0.5	2.1
1987	1.1	0.7	0.3	2.1
1988	0.7	0.6	0.3	1.6
1989	0.5	0.3	0.3	1.1
1990	0.3	0.3	0.2	0.8
TOTAL	4.0	2.1	1.6	7.7

152.   With free access to their future capital receipts and less rigid central control over capital spending generally there should be no need for well managed Category A authorities to increase their external borrowing for housing purposes. Estimates suggest that local authorities in England have over 60,000 acres of land surplus to their forseeable requirements (this figure excludes smallholdings). Even in London, there are worthwhile opportunities for turning derelict land into cash. One Inner London borough examined by auditors recently had vacant and potentially vacant land reserves of 87 acres on 140 sites. Selling this land would bring other hidden benefits in addition to cash from the sale; urban vacant sites are expensive to protect and can all too easily become a haven for crime. In addition, the subsequent use of the site generates employment.

ENCOURAGING PARTNERSHIPS BETWEEN PUBLIC AND PRIVATE SECTORS

153.   With a capital expenditure backlog on existing council stock of £20 billion or more and annual Housing Investment Programme (HIP) allocation of under £2 billion, new sources of funds must be exploited if the situation is not to deteriorate further. As the recent spate of new issues and corporate mergers has shown, there is no shortage of private money for investment in projects providing competitive real returns. The *right-to-buy* legislation is, in effect, attracting private funds into public housing: Building Societies are funding the mortgage payments which are then available (within the present control regime) for the local authority to use. However, there is a limit to what the *right-to-buy* policy can be expected to achieve – particularly if authorities are not able to reinvest more than a small part of the sale proceeds in local housing improvements. In particular, there will always be tenants who, for one reason or another, will either not want to or not be able to afford to buy their own home – even with the deep discounts (of up to 60%) now on offer:

– Some three million council tenants receiving housing benefit could not be expected to keep up mortgage payments and maintain the property even if they could secure a mortgage.

– The recent DOE report on the state of council housing showed that literally millions of council dwellings are not attractive to would-be purchasers because of their condition.

The fact that promotion of house-ownership is not necessarily a complete answer to the present crisis in public housing should not come as any surprise. As Table 25 below shows, in almost every major Western economy there is a large public and private rented sector.

Table 25: HOUSING TENURE IN SELECTED COUNTRIES
% Households living in rented accommodation (1981 except where shown)

	Private Landlord	Public Housing	Total Rented
United States	—	—	35
West Germany (1978)	—	—	63
France (1978)	—	—	44
Italy	—	—	36
Netherlands	13	43	56
Great Britain	12	30	42

Source: *National Housing Finance Systems*, Boleat (Croom Helm, 1985)

154. In the absence of direct public investment in council housing, a way of attracting private finance into public sector housing must be found if the present problems in Category B and C authorities are to be tackled effectively. The March 1985 issue of *Public Finance and Accountancy* described some of the possibilities:

(a) Building licences granted to developers by the owner of the land. The authority assembles the site, agrees the development plans and selling prices (including land values); the developer pays a small deposit (e.g. £100 a house), builds and markets the property within a specified time (usually two years) and at an agreed price, with the authority selling the land direct to the purchaser. In this way the freehold is not at any time held by the developer, thus keeping site financing costs down. London Docklands is the best known example of this approach; but over 50 local authorities have some successful experience of building under licence. Often, the authority agrees with the developer a mix of housing: refurbished dwellings for rent or shared ownership, combined with houses built for sale. In many cases, the authority retains the right to nominate tenants to the refurbished dwellings.

(b) Privately-funded shared ownership. There is apparently very substantial latent demand for some form of shared ownership, where the purchasers buy a share of a property and rent the remainder with the option to increase their share later. For example, in 1984–85 nearly 3,000 new homes were completed in Milton Keynes of which more than 800 (27%) were for shared ownership: purchasers of these properties bought a 40% share on average, and rented the remainder from the Development Corporation. Building Societies have recently developed schemes for financing the development of shared ownership housing. The Halifax Building Society recently (October 1985) issued £15 million of 3.875% index-linked 1986/2020 stock at £99 with a right to make further issues. £10 million of the proceeds has been earmarked for Milton Keynes shared ownership housing through the Milton Keynes Housing Association, which develops housing on Milton Keynes Development Corporation (MKDC) land. The scheme would work as follows, on a house costing £30,000:

Source of Funds	*Proceeds*
Building Society grants a 25-year 100% mortgage on the 50% share purchased, and takes a charge against the lease. The mortgage is covered by a financial loss guarantee from MKDC.	£15,000

MK Housing Association borrows index-linked finance from the Halifax by way of a 35-year annuity at a fixed interest rate of 4.5%. The outstanding principal is revalued annually, in accordance with the RPI and a new annuity calculated.	£10,000
MK Development Corporation treats the site value as a deferred charge to the Housing Association. It is fixed as a proportion of the market value and will be discharged either at the end of the 35-year loan or when the shared owner exercises the option to acquire 100%.	£5,000

The Housing Association leases its share to the shared owner at a rate which is re-calculated each year in line with the RPI. Initial weekly costs are estimated at £42, net of relief on the £15,000 traditional mortgage.

(c) Joint venture development between the local authority and a private development company for refurbishment of rundown property and sale as low-cost housing. One scheme (in Edinburgh) for refurbishing a 23-storey block of flats was entirely self-financing and took 18 months to complete. The only alternative open to the council was demolition. Instead, the joint venture enabled the council to liquidate its outstanding debt on the property via sale of the freehold to the developer and a share (one third of the profit on the sale of the flats which were priced in the range of £9,250 – £10,250 in 1981–82). Portsmouth has recently entered into an agreement with a builder to refurbish a problem estate which it could not afford to upgrade with its own resources without undue distortion to local priorities. Milton Keynes Development Corporation and the local council are jointly converting difficult-to-let blocks of flats to multi-occupation single person accommodation for rent.

(d) Commercial mortgages raised by tenants' co-operatives, i.e. co-ownership. This is at present under consideration in Glasgow. Tenants would be responsible for all aspects of property management for one or more blocks of flats or groups of houses; and the co-operative (not the tenants) would own the property which would be financed by a mortgage (at commercial rates) from a building society or bank guaranteed by the City Council. All refurbishment works, mortgage repayments and general expenditure not met from grant would come from rents; there will be no deficit financing. A similar scheme is being discussed by an English authority with Building Societies and Housing Associations, to provide privately-funded rental housing based on index-linked funding with a co-ownership society giving assured tenancies.

(e) Index-linked mortgages, such as have been developed for use in the London Docklands with the support of a number of pension funds. Here the interest is around half the Building Society rate; but when the dwelling is sold, three-quarters of the capital gain on the original loan is appropriated by the lender. This is a variant on the scheme that has been introduced by Nationwide: interest is charged at 4% and each year the balance outstanding and the monthly repayment is inflated by the movement in the RPI. Such schemes apparently leave everyone happy: the Pension Funds earn returns better than those on index-linked gilts and indeed much better than those on commercial property (where real returns recently have been small).

The risk to the tenant is reduced, because interest payments in the early years of the mortgage are not so great, and they are able to draw down the proceeds of the eventual capital gain while occupying the property. This approach is especially relevant in London where house prices are often too high to be affordable by first-time buyers in particular.

Local authorities will want to evaluate the potential for similar schemes locally, taking into account the scale of the investment backlog and the extent of local capital resources. Some estimates suggest that the Building Societies alone could be prepared to invest up to £1 billion a year in low-cost rented accommodation provided that competitive real returns are achievable at acceptable risks. Likewise, government will want to assess the longer-term implications for public expenditure of widespread adoption of such schemes.

155. The Commission notes that relatively few authorities appear to have followed the leads given by these projects. The author of the article referred to above reports that reaction to its theme – that partnership between public and private sectors is both necessary and desirable if the crisis in public housing is to be managed more effectively – has been underwhelming to say the least: 'It is politically sensitive you know; some councils would prefer to pull buildings down rather than involve the private sector; others, at the other end of the political spectrum, are not interested in public housing anyway – they simply want to sell'. Such attitudes are particularly unfortunate, because experience in North America, e.g. in Atlanta, Baltimore, Cleveland, Detroit, Minneapolis, New York and Washington DC, suggests that only with a productive partnership between public and private sectors can the problems of inner cities in particular be addressed.

156. A co-operative approach between the public and private sector is being applied, successfully and on a large scale, in Glasgow and in London's Docklands for instance – in each case with significant increase in public as well as private investment. The Commission expects that most Category B authorities would be able to tackle their local housing problems without the need for increased central support, given a combination of sound management and access both to future capital receipts and a willingness to tap available private sector finance.

INCREASING PUBLIC SUPPORT FOR PROBLEM AUTHORITIES

157. A combination of a shortage of housing, lack of local resources and an escalating backlog of capital maintenance on existing stock means that the steps outlined above will not be adequate to meet the needs of many problem (i.e. Category C) authorities – particularly since, by definition, none of them is notably well managed. In all these authorities, if the local housing problems are going to be tackled effectively, further public support is likely to be needed – if only (as stated above) to attract the necessary weight of private sector finance. It is not for the Commission to determine the amounts required or how they should be applied. These are matters of national and local housing policy. The options are, broadly: direct action by central government, e.g. via rate support grant, housing subsidies or Urban Programme grants; more borrowing by the local authorities to finance the necessary construction work; and the use of tax incentives to attract private funding into inner cities. The three options have important (and different) implications for the level of public expenditure now and in the future; and there will be differing views about their relative effectiveness in management terms.

158. A detailed assessment of these options is not within the scope of this report, which is directed to the management of local authority housing.

However, the Commission believes that the case for the use of tax incentives to attract private funding into inner cities warrants serious examination.

159. The challenge is how to structure housing investment packages to provide returns comparable with those available on index-linked securities. Conceptually, the problem does not appear to be insuperable, although the present system of rent controls obviously reduces the scope for attracting private finance into public housing. The Commission is aware of a number of suggestions that tax incentives for either the lenders or the borrowers might serve to increase the relative attractiveness of investment in public sector housing. For example:

- Authorities or building societies might be allowed to issue tax free bonds to fund low interest mortgages in selected problem areas.
- Rate relief might be granted in selected rundown inner-city areas (as for Enterprise Zones) with VAT relief on major refurbishment and conversions in these same areas.
- Capital allowances could be made available for residential investments under the assured tenancy's provisions.
- Current tenants in Category C areas might be able to apply their right-to-buy discount on their present home to any house of their choice, thus helping to reduce the need for new build in housing shortage areas.

But these are all proposals requiring more public investment. Unless the rate of public investment (direct or indirect) in housing stress areas is increased above the levels apparently now planned, the public and private sectors must find new ways to work productively together if building work on the scale required is to be set in hand as promptly as the situation requires.

160. In any event, it is obviously desirable to concentrate the available public support on those areas that need it most. However, at present, 35% of the HIP allocations are to authorities with negative housing Z-scores; and almost £800 million in borrowing approvals is being allocated to authorities who should be able to deal with their local housing problems without the need for additional long-term borrowing. Moreover, as Exhibit 20 shows, between 1981–82 and 1985–86 the total of rate support grant, housing subsidy and urban programme grants received by authorities with the most difficult housing problems (i.e. with a housing Z-score of 2 or more) fell almost as fast as in other authorities; in absolute terms, the total housing subsidy and urban programme grant per council dwelling fell most in the most deprived authorities. Further, capital allocations for housing have fallen every year for the past 3 years; in the current year total HIP allocations to authorities with housing Z-scores of 2 or more are over 18% lower than in 1984–85, in real terms.

161. Of course there is no point in 'throwing public money' at local housing problems, however serious, if local management is not competent to put it to good use. Fortunately, most local housing authorities with high housing Z-scores are managing their housing stock reasonably well in difficult circumstances; and many of the difficulties have been introduced by central government – misguided design standards, restrictive rent controls and the transfer of responsibility for housing benefit administration, to name but three. But in some, very few, authorities the performance of local management gives serious cause for concern. The table below classifies current relative management performance of all authorities with a housing Z-score of plus 2 or more – i.e. the more deprived authorities in housing terms. The classification is based on the analyses described in Appendix B. A Management Performance Index (MPI) of 1.4 or lower is

regarded as indicative of good management performance; authorities with an MPI of over 2 are regarded as poorly managed – such a score suggests that, on average, these authorities' performance is about half as economic, efficient or effective as the relevant 'good practice' authorities facing similar external problems. Authorities whose MPI falls between these two extremes have been classified as having moderate management performance.

Exhibit 20

TRENDS IN GRANT SUPPORT, FY 1982-1986
Rate support grant, housing subsidy, urban programme grants
£ million, at 1981 prices; Index: FY 1982 = 100

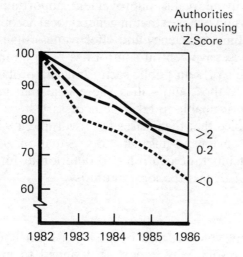

Authorities with Housing Z-Score

Real Change FY 1986 vs 1982		
Z-Score	%	£m
>2	−24	−692
0-2	−28	−428
<0	−37	−624

REDUCTION IN CENTRAL SUPPORT, FY 1986 vs 1982

Housing subsidy and urban programme

£/dwelling, at 1986 prices

Authorities with Housing Z-Score

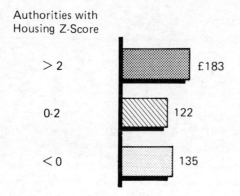

HOUSING INVESTMENT PROGRAMME ALLOCATIONS, FY 1986

£/dwelling

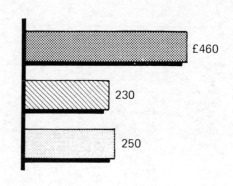

Source: Audit Commission analysis of published information, 1986

Table 26: ASSESSMENT OF RELATIVE MANAGEMENT PERFORMANCE
Authorities with housing Z-scores of over 2

	Poor	Moderate	Good	Total
London Boroughs	4	7	2	13
Metropolitan Districts	1	9	2	12
Shire Districts	1	11	9	21
TOTAL	6	27	13	46

A total of 26 authorities either did not return a questionnaire, or returned an incomplete one. Of these, six were London boroughs and one a metropolitan district. At least three of these London boroughs might be expected to fall into the poorly managed category.

162.   The recommendations of this report should enable authorities whose current management performance is moderate or poor to improve it: nothing but the best management will be good enough to tackle the serious housing problems facing this category of authority. Local reactions to auditors' work in this field over the past nine months encourages the Commission in the view that, as in other fields, authorities will take prompt action where worthwhile value improvement opportunities are shown to exist. The Commission believes that in general local accountability is a surer guarantee of economy, efficiency and effectiveness than increased central control. Indeed, excessive central control has been an important cause of many of the nation's present public sector housing problems.

163.   However, if those authorities where local management is currently poor are unwilling or unable to take the necessary steps as summarised in this report, the choice that then arises for government will be difficult and stark: allow an obviously unsatisfactory situation – but one under apparently local democratic control – to deteriorate further, throw good money after bad or bypass the local authority.

* * *

The Commission would regard bypassing a local housing authority as an action of last resort. This report is designed to make such a move unnecessary; and auditors will be continuing to work with authorities to this end. The situation will be kept under close review; a further report on progress in dealing with housing problems in inner-city areas along the lines proposed in this report will be published in due course. In the meantime, the Commission hopes that this report will serve to help and encourage local authorities and government to take prompt and effective action to deal with a crisis that threatens to get out of hand.

Appendices

A considerable amount of statistical analysis underpins the conclusions set out in the body of this report. Three appendices are included, to provide the reader with some understanding of the approach adopted by the Commission:

- Appendix A sets out the information that was collected from housing authorities and the steps taken by auditors to ensure internal consistency in the returns completed.
- Appendix B summarises the analytic approach, with the aid of a case example; it also describes how the overall housing management performance of authorities was assessed.
- Appendix C lists some of those authorities rated by the Commission as being better managed than most.

INFORMATION COLLECTED IN 1985
AUDIT COMMISSION SURVEY OF HOUSING AUTHORITIES

1.   Information on the housing function was gathered by auditors from local housing authorities in England and Wales using a detailed questionnaire. Collection of the information was carried out early in 1985, using 1983–84 as the base year. The questionnaire paid particular attention to the supervision and management aspects of housing departments, looking in particular at staffing for different functions and at related costs and workload volumes. Other information related to the size and nature of the stock, and the organisation of the housing provision in each authority.

2.   The questionnaire was designed to use information already available such as the CIPFA and HIP returns, to minimise the workload imposed on auditors and local authority staff. Auditors did however review all such sources for correctness and consistency before including the figures. Where existing sources were not available the information was obtained by detailed analysis with the co-operation of the local authority concerned. This applied particularly to the staffing figures broken down into separate headings, and to the organisation and structure of the housing function. Although this required considerable effort on the part of the authorities, for which the Commission is very grateful, in the absence of this detail it would not have been possible to carry out much of the analysis on which this report is based. Despite the considerable local effort required only 14 housing authorities did not return questionnaires, all but two of them very small shire districts (although for perhaps another 10–15 authorities the questionnaires were not fully completed).

3.   The questionnaire included precise definitions for the apportionment of staff full-time equivalents to the different functions listed. It was particularly important to identify and quantify time spent on housing functions by staff in other departments of the authority in order to make valid inter-authority comparisons possible. There were also precise definitions of, for example, what should be included in tenants' rent and rate arrears.

4.   The study team fieldwork demonstrated that there is wide diversity of accounting treatments shown in local authority Housing Revenue Accounts. It was therefore essential to ensure that all the cost information was strictly comparable. This was achieved by including in the questionnaire detailed worksheets on which auditors could make adjustments to the reported accounts where necessary. This was particularly relevant in recording special services expenditure broken down by standard headings (services for the elderly, caretaking and cleaning, maintenance of open spaces, etc.). In many authorities, the reported figures are not identified under the appropriate heading and considerable adjustment was necessary. As a result of these adjustments and the precise definitions used, the data now available represents the most accurate and reliable data source on local authority housing in England and Wales currently available. The remainder of this Appendix describes the information collected in the questionnaire.

5.   The *composition of local council-owned stock* at the end of March 1984. This was broken down in detail, as follows:
   (a)   Type of dwelling
          1, 2 and 3 bedroom dwellings:
          –   houses
          –   flats
          –   bungalows

4 or more bedroom dwellings

Other dwellings

(b) Age of building (% of total stock):
- before 1945
- 1945–1964
- after 1964

(c) Height of dwelling:
- numbers built under Housing Acts, 1 to 4 storeys
- numbers built under Housing Acts, 5 or more storeys
- numbers acquired or purchased, and other dwellings
- total dwellings

6. *Housing department organisation at end March 1984.* The questionnaire obtained the following information about the way in which the local housing service was being managed:

(a) Department responsible for each of the following housing functions:
- rent collection
- rent accounting
- arrears recovery
- repairs administration (client functions)
- DLO
- housing benefit administration for council tenants
- housing aid or advice on debt counselling (structured service)
- housing research (inc. HIP)
- management of sheltered schemes
- computer system design, input and operations.

(b) Whether housing department decentralised. If decentralised, number of area offices, sub-offices and estate management offices.

(c) Degree of decentralistion by function (fully centralised, partly decentralised, fully decentralised):
- waiting list administration
- allocation and relets
- transfer waiting list
- transfer allocations
- mutual exchanges
- rent collection
- rent accounting
- arrears: current tenants
- arrears: former tenants
- control of estate caretakers
- estate management
- management of sheltered schemes
- repair orders
- void control, inc. inspections
- housing benefit administration
- homelessness administration

(d) Computerisation of the nominal ledger, and type of management account reports.

(e) Computer use for housing functions: for each of the following whether already implemented, under development, planned for development by end 1985–86, or no plans for computerisation. (Implementation date and name of package also requested, if available):
- rent accounting/arrears
- capital and development control
- office systems, e.g., word proccesing

- waiting lists and allocations
- maintenance
- estate management
- improvement grants
- sales, inc. service charges
- mortgages
- housing benefits
- forecasting
- setting rent levels.

(f) For rent accounting, whether on-line enquiry system, and type of service.

7. Information on *general supervision and management and other costs*, and levels of service was also obtained, as follows:

(a) *Costs*. General S & M expenditure (net) as reported in abstract of accounts or revised estimate for 1983–84, as well as:
- central establishment charges, as included in general and special S & M
- insurance costs
- cost of gypsy sites (net before recharge) and number of pitches
- housing advice centres (gross costs)
- sale of dwellings administration cost, if reported (gross).

(b) *Waiting lists and allocations*. This included:
- number on housing waiting lists (including active and deferred) at 31 March 1984
- number on transfer lists at 31 March 1984
- number on mutual exchange lists at 31 March 1984
- number of new applicants to housing waiting lists 1983–84
- number of new transfer applicants 1983–84
- number of new exchange applicants 1983–84
- number of new lettings (relets) during 1983–84:
  - from waiting list
  - from transfer list
  - all exchanges (inc. NMS, TES etc.)
  - homeless
  - other
- frequency of renewal of application (6 month, annual, biennial) for both waiting and transfer list applicants
- number of visits to housing and transfer applicants on first application
- number of visits to applicants near to allocation
- offer refusal rate.

(c) *Housing advice and homelessness*, including the approximate annual number of new cases registered with housing advice centres or housing offices; the number of all homeless applications in 1983–84 and the number of homeless applications accepted as homeless and in priority need in 1983–84.

(d) *Voids*: the number of vacant properties at 1 April 1984, identifying separately those available for letting, undergoing repair or improvement, awaiting repair or improvement and awaiting sale or demolition. In addition, the questionnaire obtained information on:
- policy to inform applicants of a provisional allocation of a dwelling before the current tenant has moved out
- policy to encourage applicants to view allocated dwellings before the current tenant has moved out
- responsibility for internal redecoration on reletting:
  - the authority

- the tenant
- the tenant with monetary or other assistance from the authority
- existence of separate voids control staff
- average elapsed weeks between relets of all empty properties:
  - estimate provided by the authority
  - calculation based on average void level and number of relets.

(e) *Repairs*. Proportion of maintenance expenditure carried out by DLO and contractors; and the approximate annual number of repair job tickets.

(f) *Sale of dwellings*. Number of *right-to-buy* applications received during 1983–84 and percentage of admitted claims withdrawn (after Section 10 offers) as well as the number of completed sales during 1983–84 and the percentage of leasehold sales of total sales.

(g) *Rent collection*. Number of dwellings collected by various methods, and frequency of collection:
- cash offices
- door to door
- Post Office Giro (all methods)
- banker's order, direct debit and credit transfer
- other methods (e.g. deduction from pay)
- housing benefit cases making no additional payment
- total dwellings let (excluding voids).

(h) *Arrears*. Current and former tenants' arrears at 31 March 1984 and number of accounts were identified separately. In addition, information was obtained on:
- annual gross and net debits 1983–84
- policy on rent free weeks
- frequency of update of tenants' accounts
- number of cash offices, both full and part time.

(i) *Housing benefit*. In addition to information on the average number of local authority tenants receiving rent rebates (certificated and standard), the questionnaire covered:
- number of successful new applications for rent rebates: local authority tenants (certificated and standard)
- gross costs of rent rebate administration for local authority tenants for 1983–84:
  - staff
  - total

(j) Subjective rating of degree of commitment to 'estate management' in terms of a checklist of activities typically carried out by 'estate management' staff.

8. Information on *special services costs* and volumes was obtained. This covered:

(a) Gross costs adjusted as necessary in accordance with defined procedure:
- central heating
- community centres
- lighting of staircases, corridors, etc.
- lifts
- cleaning only services (i.e. without caretaking)
- caretaking and cleaning (combined service)
- services for the elderly
- maintenance of HRA open spaces
- communal laundry and other communal services

- other special S & M expenditure
- provision for the homeless (inc. bed and breakfast)
(b) Central heating income.
(c) Service charges for sheltered schemes for warden's services (excluding rent and central heating charges).
(d) Gross expenditure on bed and breakfast accommodation for the homeless.
(e) Number of dwellings provided with:
  - central heating (landlord controlled)
  - communal lighting
  - caretaking
  - cleaning only, without caretaking (exc. sheltered blocks).
(f) Services for the elderly:
  - number of dwellings controlled exclusively by central alarm station and/or mobile wardens or other domiciliary peripatetic services for the elderly
  - number of dwellings controlled solely by mobile wardens (with no central alarm station)
  - number of sheltered dwellings (e.g. category 1 and 2) with resident wardens (other than part $2\frac{1}{2}$)
  - number of part $2\frac{1}{2}$ dwellings (very sheltered)
  - average block size (category 1 and 2 and part $2\frac{1}{2}$ schemes with resident wardens).
(g) Homelessness: Number of homeless household nights in accommodation provided by the council:
  - hostels
  - bed and breakfast
  - other (e.g. difficult to let or short life property)
  - hostel capacity (units)
(h) Other data was also collected under this heading, including the number of community centres, hectarage of housing open spaces and number of lifts in all council dwellings, (excluding stair lifts).

9. Full-time equivalent *staff establishment engaged on housing functions* at 31 March 1984. The number of staff engaged and the department responsible were identified for the following functions:
(a) *Waiting lists*: all facets of the administration of the general waiting list, transfer/exchange lists, other waiting lists, nominations and mobility schemes. This heading included the receipt, processing and recording of new applications and renewals, including all correspondence, visiting and interviewing for the purpose of assessing priorities for inclusion of applicants on the waiting list(s).
(b) *Allocations and lettings*: the selection and matching of applicants to particular dwellings, interviewing and making offers of accommodation, arranging supply of keys and viewing of property, granting tenancy and explaining conditions for all new lettings and relets.
(c) *Rent collection*: all aspects of rent collection (other than arrears chasing) up to and including balancing of strips, etc. Staff on door-to-door and cash office/other collections should be allocated separately and recorded under their respective departments. Any apportionment of the time of cash office staff should be for public sector rent/rates only and should not include staff time for private rates or other payments.
(d) *Rent accounting*: the reconciliation of cash receipts, balancing individual tenants' accounts, transfer of office, door-to-door, Giro, etc, collections to manual accounting system and balancing, recording indebtedness of individual tenants and production of new

strips where appropriate. Rent accounting included dealing with routine tenants' account queries. Where computer systems are employed, rent accounting included transfer of data to input forms and/or inputting data via computer terminals. Rent accounting also covered the maintenance of the gross housing debit, including dealing with individual debit amendments. Specialist computer staff were not to be included.

(e) *Rent arrears recovery*: staff requirements for the identification of arrears cases requiring remedial action, implementing control procedures such as 'arrears' letters; visiting and interviewing of arrears cases at home, and production of visit reports. Where interviews are conducted at head office, this was included. Arrears control included advising tenants generally on the availability of benefits and debt counselling, but excluded benefits administration. Attendance at arrears committees or at court should not have been included where this is a senior management responsibility – see under General Management.

(f) *Housing benefits administration*: the staff requirement by department for local authority tenants only, including as appropriate receipt of application, verification, interviewing, assessing, granting, etc. The recording of benefit changes in the individual tenants' account or in the gross housing debit falls within rent accounting. Work in respect of private tenants and owner-occupiers was excluded. The staff should be as shown on DHSS form MPF 673, section 5, part k(i) column 1.

(g) *Repairs administration (client element)*: staff requirements for repairs up to placement of job orders to the appropriate department and/or contractor and overall progress control of repairs jobs up to completion. This included all pre-inspection of jobs/dwellings to specify work to be undertaken, authorisation of such work, selection of contractors, administration of rechargeable items and maintenance of appropriate records. Post-inspection, quality control, and planned maintenance programmes, should not have been included; neither should maintenance operatives.

(h) *Management of services for the elderly*: time devoted by officers to managing sheltered schemes, part $2\frac{1}{2}$ schemes and OAP dwellings without wardens but connected to central alarm systems: it also included management of any itinerant or visiting warden service. Actual wardens and cleaners at sheltered schemes or central alarm stations were included under (u) below.

(i) *Void control*: the staff time spent on visiting properties which are, or are about to become void, and on the control of voids (i.e., records and statistics).

(j) *Estate management*: all facets of estate upkeep, including tenancy conditions, lodgers, garden maintenance, parking of vehicles, neighbour disputes, liaison with tenants' associations, other day-to-day advice. It also included home visiting of tenants by the estates' staff on either an intermittent or regular basis other than for arrears work or for void inspections. Supervision of caretaking staff was included, but actual caretaking staff were not. Estate management included routine inspections of dwellings and estates, but excluded repairs administration (see (g) above).

(k) *Housing welfare*: any specialist staff dealing with domestic disputes, marital problems, home economics, co-ordination with social services and home visiting specifically related to welfare problems.

90

(l) *Homelessness administration*: staff dealing with potential or actual cases of homelessness in the public and private sectors. This included visiting, interviewing, assessing applications, correspondence and statistics, and co-ordination with other authorities. It did not include hostel wardens or cleaners, or senior management attendance at committee, working groups, etc. – see under general management.

(m) *Administration*: all typing, filing, telephone and other support services for the housing department plus staff dealing with supplies, accounts, budgets, personnel records, salaries, wages, etc.

(n) *Research and systems*: where applicable this included liaison with computer personnel and housing research.

(o) *General management*: the senior or 'higher' management of the department (normally the first and second tier in the organisation). This included staff responsible for housing policy matters, mix requirements, building programmes, councillors' or MPs' queries/ interviews, attendance at committees, working groups, court, management teams, public speaking or lecturing and day-to-day control of the department and implementation of council policy.

(p) *Capital project management*: housing staff requirements for the management of all clearance and/or modernisation programmes. This included modernisation and rehabilitation of dwellings, administration of clearance areas, liaison with public utilities and decanting requirements for any of the foregoing. Where any of these functions was entirely outside the scope of the housing department, no allowance was included in the apportionment.

(q) *Housing aid/advice*: a structured housing aid or advisory service. Day-to-day advice may be given, *ad hoc*, by any member of staff; and apportionment of such time was not required. Housing advisers for the elderly were included.

(r) *Sale of council houses*: all aspects of the sale of council dwellings from initial enquiry to handover of property to the purchaser. Staff of other departments were included and recorded under their respective departments.

(s) *Trainees*: staff specifically designated and operating as trainees within the establishment or supernumerary to the establishment.

(t) *Caretakers*: excluded all homeless hostel staff, and all staff as sheltered or other accommodation for the elderly.

(u) *Sheltered wardens and cleaners*: included central alarm station staff, mobile and/or itinerant wardens and staff at Category 1 and 2 and Part $2\frac{1}{2}$ schemes.

(v) *Hostel staff*: wardens and cleaners at homeless hostels.

(w) *Cleaners*: other than those at homeless hostels or accommodation for the elderly.

(x) *Other functions*: all staff not apportioned to the specific functions itemised above, e.g. staff engaged on post-inspection for maintenance or housing staff engaged on improvement grants or non-HRA mortgages. (The staff were not included in the analysis.)

* * *

It will be evident that very detailed and consistent information of high quality was gathered from a large number of housing authorities. This formed the basis for the analysis of housing management performances and underpins the proposed performance benchmarks and overall ratings of different authorities housing management, as described in Appendix B.

ANALYSIS OF THE SURVEY DATA

1. This appendix describes the method of analysis of the questionnaire data, illustrated by an example relating to the staffing levels for the administration of the waiting and transfer lists. Similar analysis was carried out for a total of 17 cost or staffing elements of the housing function. The appendix also describes the way in which the results of the analysis were combined to produce the overall index of management performance discussed in Chapter 4 of the main report.

STATISTICAL APPROACH

2. In addition to providing material for the report, the main purpose of the analysis was to provide authorities with a means of assessing their performance in direct comparison with similar authorities. Conceptually, the problem is very complex since a large number of factors outside authorities' immediate control might well influence their housing management performance. To take a relatively straightforward example, the level of rent arrears can be shown to be affected by such factors as the amount of stock that the authority has to manage, whether door-to-door rent collection is used, and local socio-economic conditions such as the number of recipients of housing benefit.

3. It is therefore not possible to establish a simple benchmark of good performance, except as a relatively crude, first level, indicator. In some cases, rent and rate arrears of 2% of gross debit could be regarded as relatively poor performance; and in others, arrears of, say, 6% might be regarded as reasonable in light of the local circumstances. The Commission has therefore had to use the data in the questionnaire to develop for each individual authority some indicators to show how its performance relates to reasonable expectations given the relevant local circumstances, on the following elements of housing management:

(a) Void control: proportion of voids, and staffing.
(b) Arrears recovery: proportion of gross debit, and staffing.
(c) Waiting and transfer list staff.
(d) Lettings (allocation) staff.
(e) Rent collection staff (door-to-door and cash office).
(f) Rent accounting staff.
(g) Sale of dwellings: staff and cost.
(h) Services for the elderly: staff and cost.
(i) Homelessness administration staff.
(j) Housing advice centre staff.
(k) Housing benefit administration staff.
(l) Cost of maintaining open spaces.

4. The indicators were developed using a computer-assisted statistical technique known as multiple regression analysis. The purpose of the regression analysis is to establish the extent of the correlation between the variations from authority to authority in staff numbers engaged in a function and other factors, both within and outside an authority's control. Examples of factors under the control of the authority would include policy decisions for instance on waiting list renewals and rent levels, management organisation, methods of rent collection and the use of computers. Examples of factors outside the authority's control would include the size and mix of their housing stock, the number of waiting list applications received, the nature of the housing stock (in the short-term at least) as well as the characteristics of the population at large, e.g. from Census data.

5. For each element, the analysis is carried out on all the data available, in order to identify which factors are associated with different numbers of

staff. More specifically, the regression analyses seek to quantify the effect of a change in any specified factor on the number of staff actually employed by an authority. For example, it may be shown that the greater the social deprivation of an area, the more staff are required to administer the waiting list. An authority with higher-than-average social deprivation might then be expected to have higher-than-average staffing per 1,000 on the list, all other things being equal. [This may not always be the case, however. As a result of good management, an authority may still be able to operate the list satisfactorily with fewer staff than might be expected by comparison with others].

6. Having established and quantified the relationship between staffing and these other factors using data from all authorities – in effect the 'average' staffing level – it is possible to identify those authorities that perform better than expected, i.e. those with below-average staff for a given set of circumstances. The procedure then is to repeat the regression analysis on this reduced set of data (approximately 50% of authorities) to establish what it is about these authorities that enables them to operate with below-average staff. A new average is then determined for these authorities, corresponding approximately to the level of the best 25% overall. This is termed the 'good practice' level. Of course, a simple average would not be an adequate measure with which to compare an authority's performance. The advantage of regression analysis is that it enables account to be taken of many different factors at the same time, quantifying the effect of each. Although the results can therefore be described in terms of averages, the resulting performance indicator is much more useful for making inter-authority comparisons *given the relevant adjustments for factors outside the authority's control.* Table B-1 summarises these factors that have emerged from the regression analysis and have been taken into account in evaluating the various elements of authorities' housing management performance:

Table B-1: RELEVANT FACTORS INCORPORATED INTO PERFORMANCE INDICATORS

Element of Housing Management	Most Relevant Factors
Void control	% dwellings over 4 storeys % work performed by DLO Pre-allocation policy Shaw classification
Arrears control	Number of dwellings let Rent collection method Shaw classification
Waiting and transfer list staffing	Number of applications Number of visits to applicants Number of ethnic minority households
Letting staff	Number of offers made
Rent collection staff	Number of collections
Rent accounting staff	Number of new lets
Sales of dwellings, staff	Number of freehold and leasehold sales
Cost of sheltered accommodation	Mix of services (alarms, wardens, dwellings) Block size
Homelessness administration staff	Number of applicants Total dwellings with shared amenities
Housing benefit administration staff	Local authority recipients of rent and rate rebates
Maintenance of open spaces, cost	Mix of authority stock (i.e. number of dwellings in flats over 4 storeys, up to and including 4 storeys and all other dwellings).

EXAMPLE: WAITING LIST ADMINISTRATION

7. The first step is to draw up a list of all the factors which those familiar with the practical realities of administering council house waiting lists consider may have some effect on staffing for waiting list administration. These fall into three groups:

(a) internal (controllable) factors
- number and frequency of visits to applicants
- procedure for renewing the list
- degree of computerisation
- organisation of housing function

(b) internal (uncontrollable) factors
- number of offers
- offer refusal rate
- number on waiting and transfer list
- number of applications to waiting and transfer list
- number of relets

(c) external factors (Census data)
- number of overcrowded households
- number of large families
- number of households of ethnic origin
- number of migrants
- Shaw classification

8. Each of these factors may be of significance in determining the work volume, and hence the required staffing for waiting list administration. It may not be necessary, however, to include all the factors in the regression analysis. In fact, it is preferable to have fewer if possible for ease of interpretation of the results. If it can be shown that there is an association between a pair of factors (in statistical terms an 'auto-correlation') then there would be an element of double-counting in the regression if both were included. One of the pair is dropped leaving the other to explain variations in staffing. An example of this might be a high correlation between 'overcrowding' and 'large families'. It is possible to calculate the correlations between all pairs of the factors and also between each factor and the actual staff used. The set of factors used in regression analysis should be those with high correlation with staffing (i.e. those which explain as much as possible of the variation in staffing at different authorities) but low correlation with each other.

9. From the above list it was established that the most important factor affecting waiting list administration staffing is (not surprisingly perhaps) the number of applications received. Also relatively important are the number of visits made on application, and a demographic factor: the number of households of ethnic origin.

10. However, the factors must be interpreted with care. A variable such as the number of applications is easy to understand as a straightforward volume measure of workload, i.e. an increase in the number of applications can be expected to require additional staff. But the Census variables on the other hand cannot be translated directly to staffing in the same way. An increase in, say, the proportion of ethnic families might be associated with an increase in the work required to process each application. This does not mean that only ethnic families produce this effect – this variable is simply a 'proxy' for perhaps many other social factors.

11. The statistical method enables all possible combinations of explanatory factors to be evaluated. The most important are then selected and the effect of each is quantified by computer, repeating the process on the 'below average' authorities for each element analysed, for each authority in turn. The 'good practice' indicator for waiting list administration staffing in each authority therefore takes account of the relevant characteristics of the

individual authority. This can be compared directly with the authority's actual staffing (or cost). If the actual figure is above the indicator then the auditor and the authority can together investigate the reasons, and identify the scope for possible improvement.

12.   Using the example of waiting list administration, the staffing levels for every authority were predicted, taking into account the relevant factors: number of applications received, number of visits allowed per applicant [a local policy matter] and the proportion of households where the head was born in the new Commonwealth. The predicted staffing level can then be compared with the actual level, using the following equation developed from the multiple regression analysis.

Full-time equivalent staffing for waiting and transfer list administration
$$= [(0.865 \times a) + (0.862 \times b) + (0.164 \times c)]$$
where: a = total annual applications received
b = total number of visits to applicants
c = number of households where the head was born in the new Commonwealth – a proxy for urban deprivation.

13.   A similar approach was taken for all the elements of housing management listed in paragraph 3 above. Thus, with this information, individual authorities have been able to review their performance on different elements of housing management, taking the most relevant local external factors into account. This list does not cover every activity of the housing function – consideration of repairs administration, for example, has been deferred until the Commission's report on housing maintenance later this year. Other activities such as administrative support are not included because the data was not suitable for regression analysis – indicators based on the Shaw classification have been used instead.

OVERALL ASSESSMENT OF AUTHORITIES' PERFORMANCE

14.   The various indicators enable the Commission to review authorities' performance in relation to each function individually. These indicators were subsequently combined to produce a single Management Performance Index (MPI) which could be used to compare all authorities' performance overall. This index is directly comparable from authority to authority, since it has been derived from the series of indicators each of which takes account of an authority's own special circumstances. (The voids indicator allows for the proportion of high-rise flats, for example, and the arrears indicator for the proportion of rent collected door-to-door.) For each authority, for each element, a ratio was calculated of the actual staff (or cost) to the good practice indicator staff (or cost). Thus a ratio of 1 would show that the authority was at the good practice level for that function. A ratio of less than 1 would show that the authority was performing very well, while a ratio of, say, 2 would show that the authority had twice the staff (or expenditure) on a particular function than would be expected if it performed at the level of its more efficient peers, *making due allowances* for its special circumstances.

This is illustrated in Exhibit B–1 which shows, for each authority, the ratio of actual staff to 'good practice' staff. Authorities to the left of the line are doing better than might be expected given the local circumstances.

15.   Each individual indicator was then weighted to reflect its level of importance for potential economy, efficiency and effectiveness improvements. Clearly, for example, the potential benefit of a reduction in void levels as described in Chapter Two would outweigh the benefit of a reduction in staff engaged in the sale of dwellings. Weights were therefore determined in relation to the financial effect of an improvement in each element as shown in the report. Table B–2 summarises the weights applied to the various factors.

Exhibit B-1

WAITING AND TRANSFER LIST ADMINISTRATION
Ratio of actual staff to "good practice" staff

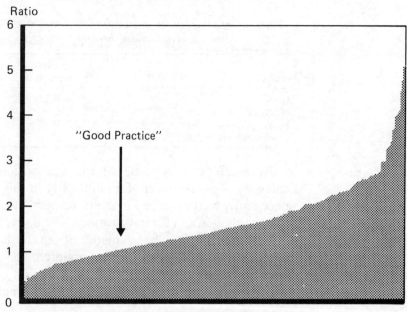

Source: Audit Commission Survey, 1985

Table B–2: WEIGHTING FACTORS APPLIED

Performance Factor	Weighting
Void control	25
Arrears control	13
Cost of housing services for the elderly	12
Cost of open spaces maintenance	10
Housing benefit administration staff	9
Cost of rent collection staff [as appropriate]	
– door-to-door	5
– cash office	4
Cost of rent accounting staff	5
Cost of council house sales staff	5
Others factors (4)	12
	100

16.   Each ratio was then multiplied by the corresponding weight and then aggregated across all the elements for each authority. The resulting Management Performance Index for the authority is in effect its average performance compared with relevant good practice across the whole range of elements of housing management examined. The index can thus be used to make direct comparisons between authorities in terms of overall management performance on the following basis:

(a)   Authorities with an index of 1.4 or better (i.e. less) can be regarded as having good management performance: this score implies that on most elements, their performance is not far out of line with good practice taking the relevant external factors into account.

(b)   Authorities with an MPI greater than 2 were regarded as having poor management performance. This score implies that on average, their performance on the various elements of housing management is half the benchmark level, taking relevant local factors into account.

(c)   Authorities falling between the two extremes were classified as having moderate performance.

97

Table B–3 summarises the results, by class of authority, for all those authorities covered in the analysis. The authorities excluded either did not return a questionnaire or the questionnaire was not sufficiently complete for a full analysis.

Table B–3:   SUMMARY OF PERFORMANCE ASSESSMENT RESULTS
Number of Authorities Surveyed

Assessment	Shire Districts	Met. Districts	London Boroughs	Total
Good	101 (30%)	14 (39%)	5 (20%)	120 (31%)
Moderate	182	19	16	217
Poor	31	2	5	38
[Authorities not included in assessment	19	1	6]	26

Appendix C lists some of the authorities in the good management category. The inclusion of an authority in this list does not imply that it is necessarily well managed in every respect. Even the best authority is likely to have some room for improvement. Equally, as discussed in paragraph 13, no assessment has been made of an authority's performance in the administration of repairs, or its maintenance performance generally. The MPI does, however, serve to draw attention to particular authorities from which others can draw examples of good practice.

Appendix C

LIST OF WELL-MANAGED HOUSING AUTHORITIES

1. It is not the Commission's practice to issue performance league tables – not least because of the need to take account of the many factors outside authorities' immediate or direct control which inevitably affects their relative performance. In addition, the Commission and its auditors are not at liberty to publish information gained in the course of an audit without the permission of the authority in question, under Section 30 of the *Local Government Finance Act, 1982*.

2. However, there is merit in publishing – of course with their permission – the names of those authorities where analysis suggests that housing management performance is generally better than most, taking relevant factors into account:

(a) Authorities learn most from each other rather than from published reports and central 'guidance'. It is members asking the question, 'if they can do it in X, why can't we?' that constitutes the most powerful stimulant to local action. It is therefore very important that members of housing authorities can identify some near neighbours who apparently are doing rather better than their circumstances might suggest to be possible – for management reasons.

(b) When good practice in a particular authority is commended in the body of the report, a reader is entitled to enquire whether the performance of the authority in question stands up to objective scrutiny. It is not unknown for authorities to 'talk a good game'.

For both these reasons, the Commission deemed it appropriate to list those authorities whose housing management performance is generally better than most.

3. The following table therefore lists examples of the authorities of all types whose overall housing management performance is rated as good as described in Appendix B. All the authorities shown have agreed to be identified. The authorities within each category are listed in housing Z-score order, with the most deprived in housing terms listed first.

*   *   *

Even authorities which are judged to be well-managed overall in housing terms, such as those listed over the page, can still have room for improvement in particular functions. (Auditors will be following up any outstanding matters.) Equally, a well-managed housing function does not necessarily imply that all other services are of the same standard.

Table C–1: WELL-MANAGED HOUSING AUTHORITIES AS ASSESSED BY THE AUDIT COMMISSION

Shire Districts		Met. Districts	London Boroughs
Blackburn	Charnwood	Birmingham	Kensington & Chelsea
Nottingham	North Devon	Salford	Hounslow
Merthyr Tydfil	Hereford	Bolton	Barnet
Preston	Amber Valley	Sunderland	Kingston
Cynon Valley	Tynedale	Doncaster	
Hove	E. Cambridgeshire	Wigan	
Rossendale	New Forest	Barnsley	
Rhymney Valley	Stafford	Sefton	
Wear Valley	Broxtowe	Stockport	
Hartlepool	N. E. Derbyshire	Solihull	
Penwith	Windsor & Maidenhead		
Southampton	East Yorkshire		
Islwyn	Cherwell		
Bournemouth	West Oxfordshire		
Swansea	Lewes		
Great Grimsby	Aylesbury Vale		
Torbay	Waverley		
Southend on Sea	Blaby		
E. Staffordshire	West Derbyshire		
Worcester	Horsham		
Exeter	Beverley		
Eastbourne	Luton		
Colwyn	Rochford		
Darlington	Selby		
Newcastle-under-Lyme	Chiltern		
Boston	Hart		
Havant	Richmondshire		
Colchester	Hambleton		
Durham	Ryedale		

Printed in the UK for HMSO by Linneys Colour Print
Dd. 738550. C40. 2/86. 46449